MAN

KILLED

BY

PHEASANT

and Other Kinships

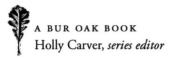

A BUR OAK BOOK

Holly Carver, *series editor*

MAN

KILLED

BY

PHEASANT

and Other Kinships

by John T. Price

UNIVERSITY OF IOWA PRESS, IOWA CITY

University of Iowa Press, Iowa City 52242
www.uiowapress.org
Copyright © 2008 by John T. Price
Originally published by Da Capo Press, 2008
First University of Iowa Press edition, 2012
Printed in the United States of America

The University of Iowa Press is a member of Green Press
Initiative and is committed to preserving natural resources.

Printed on acid-free paper

Library of Congress Cataloging-in-Publication Data
Price, John, 1966–
Man killed by pheasant: and other kinships / by John T. Price.—
1st University of Iowa Press ed.
p.   cm.—(A Bur oak book)
Originally published: Cambridge, MA: Da Capo Press, c2008.
ISBN-13: 978-1-60938-075-5, ISBN-10: 1-60938-075-4 (pbk.)
1. Price, John, 1966– —Anecdotes.   2. Price, John, 1966– —
Family—Anecdotes.   3. Price, John, 1966– —Homes and
haunts—Anecdotes.   4. Prairies—Middle West—Anecdotes.
5. Prairies—Iowa—Anecdotes.   6. Middle West—Social life and
customs—Anecdotes.   7. Iowa—Social life and customs—
Anecdotes.   8. Middle West—Biography—Anecdotes.
9. Iowa—Biography—Anecdotes.   I. Title.
CT275.P84267A3 2012   977.092— dc23
[B]   2011031853

FOR BENJAMIN AND SPENCER

CONTENTS

Acknowledgments   ix

On Haskell Street (A Prelude)   1

PART ONE—DEPARTURES
The Robin Defense   15
What Kind of Light?   19
Mole Man Lives!   43
Nymph   67
Titan   81
Night Rhythms   101

PART TWO—NEW LANDS
Love Mountain   109
High Maintenance   123
Man Killed by Pheasant   143
Prairie Asinus   153
Shoveling   169

PART THREE—HOME
Dave and the Devil   179
Nuts   203
Why Geese Don't Winter in Paradise   215
Moon Kitty   235

On Kalsow Prairie (A Postlude)   245

ACKNOWLEDGMENTS

This book, like most memoirs, weaves together history and memory. A number of historical people, however, through no fault of their own, have come to inhabit my (sometimes imperfect) memory of events. To protect the innocent I have changed names, some identifying features, and a few place names. My family has not been so fortunate. So I want to thank them, first and foremost, for their unwavering love, generosity, and patience. I owe a special debt of gratitude to my parents, Tom and Sondra Price, my sisters and their husbands—Carrie Anne and Mark Whittaker, Susan and Tim Saylor, Allyson and Jason Rushford—and all of my amazing nieces and nephews. In addition, I am grateful to my cousin David Price, and to the marvelous Strine family, especially Gary and Helen. I would also like to honor my grandparents, Roy and Mildred Price, and Harold and Kathryn Anderson, as well as my great aunt Esther Lundquist and my adopted grandfather, Lloyd Strine. Their loving hands are all over these pages.

It has been a pleasure and privilege to work with Merloyd Lawrence at Da Capo, whose vision, wisdom and encouragement made this book possible. Thank you for believing in my work! Thanks as well to my agent, Joanne Wyckoff at Zachary Shuster Harmsworth, who has long been a champion of nature writers. I also deeply appreciate the efforts of Renee Caputo and Lissa Warren at Perseus on behalf of this book. *Man Killed by Pheasant* has been over ten years in the making, and many have been generous with their time and talents. I have been blessed with a number of good, magnanimous friends whose advice and support I have relied on while completing this book. I would like to especially thank Karla Armbruster, Christopher Cokinos, Hope Edelman, Diane Horton Comer, Elmar Lueth, Michele Morano, Andy Nesler, Steve Newman, Maria Nilsson, Mary Swander, and Kathy Wallace. I would not be a writer without the guidance of my nonfiction teachers at the University of Iowa, including Paul Diehl, Carl Klaus, Carol de Saint Victor, Tom Simmons, and visiting teachers Patricia Hampl and Carol Bly. I'm also grateful for the support of my colleagues, friends, and students at the University of Nebraska at Omaha, particularly my nonfiction compadres: J.J. McKenna, Lisa Knopp, and Phil Smith. Susan Maher and Michael Skau, as chairs of the English Department, and Shelton Hendricks, Dean of the College of Arts and Sciences, provided essential assistance. I was also greatly aided by a UNO Faculty Development Fellowship and by a 2004 creative writing fellowship from the National Endowment for the Arts.

I feel fortunate to have collaborated with many gifted editors, including H. Emerson Blake and Aina Barton at *Orion*, Ladette Randolph at the University of Nebraska Press, Lee Gutkind at *Creative Nonfiction*, Christopher Cokinos at *Isotope*, and Robert

W. Lewis at *North Dakota Quarterly*. My profound thanks to the editors and staff at the following journals, magazines, and newspapers who published earlier versions of some of the chapters: *Orion* ("Man Killed By Pheasant," "Nuts," "High Maintenance," and "Moon Kitty"), *Creative Nonfiction* ("Night Rhythms"), *Isotope: A Journal of Literary Nature and Science Writing* ("Why Geese Don't Winter in Paradise"), *The Christian Science Monitor* ("Shoveling"), and *North Dakota Quarterly* ("On Haskell Street").

Finally, I wish to express my deepest love and gratitude to my wife, Stephanie, and to our wonderful sons, Benjamin and Spencer. Where would I be without you? Not here. Not anywhere.

*The foregoing generations beheld God and
nature face to face; we, through their eyes.*

*Why should not we also enjoy an original
relation to the universe?*

—RALPH WALDO EMERSON

On Haskell Street
(A Prelude)

———◆———

During the winters of adolescence, I would sometimes spend a Saturday or two with my great-aunt Esther. Around suppertime, she would have me run down to the grocery to purchase Swedish potato sausage and lingonberries, which she'd later serve next to white bread with thick swipes of butter on it. The rest of the evening would be spent at her piano singing a few of her father's favorite songs. Immigrant songs. Songs about forgotten children, sinful princes, and the narrow way to God's eternal dawn: *Den langa evighetens dag, i orstörd frid och ro.* That eternal day of peace and quiet. Esther would recall how her father, John, sang these songs to her and her younger brother, Harold, while rocking on the porch of their house on Haskell Street in Fort Dodge, in west-central Iowa. Tillie, their mother, would step away from the sewing table to add her birdlike soprano to a few verses. Sometimes, said Esther, upon hearing John's voice, immigrant neighbors like Mrs. Samuelson and Josey would wander over to join them on the porch. Little Josey, who'd had a baby at fourteen, refused to nurse it and called out instead for her puppy dog, Snips.

1

"*Sjung en visa för oss*, John!" Josey would demand, scratching the mutt's neck: "Sing a story for us!"

By the time of these visits to Aunt Esther's all the family members who'd ever lived on Haskell Street had died or moved away. John and Tillie had died decades before I was born. Esther lived in Boone, sixty miles away, and her brother Harold "Andy" Anderson, my maternal grandfather, had uprooted to Arizona when I was nine. My friends didn't come from around Haskell Street, set in the Des Moines River valley, which I mostly viewed while driving across Kenyon Road bridge—the forested bluffs, the abandoned roundhouse, the small overflow dam where shirtless boys cast their lines into the foam, despite the stench of the processing plants. The "armpit" we sometimes called it. I grew up with my three younger sisters on the other side of town, where the neighborhoods were plotted in perfect squares and the well-groomed fields of corn and beans ran east to the horizon. Our house was larger than those on Haskell; our yard was a thin acre with blooming crab apples along the drive, shade gardens, climbing trees. A small park, really.

And yet it was for a child like me that my great-grandparents had left Sweden. Or so I'd been told by Grandma Kathryn, wife of Harold. "Yes," Esther would nod, "I suppose that's true. And did you also know you were born with a veil on your face, like your mother?" She was referring to some kind of gross skin mask, but according to Swedish legend it meant Mom and I were "touched," set apart for Christ, destined to save the world. Even my mother believed it. When I was seven and she was pregnant with my brother, I became very ill, feverish and delusional. The doctor speculated leukemia. *Dear God,* my mother prayed at my bedside, *let him be saved*. And so it happened: I recovered from what turned out to be a virus, but my brother, James, was stillborn. For a brief time, though, I was the answer to everyone's prayers, a miracle.

No wonder I wanted to be Swedish. While still in elementary school, I learned bits of the language from Esther—*Jag alskär dig*—and wrapped myself in the stories of John and Tillie, who I believed were circling above my head, guarding and protecting me, the one set apart. I imagined how it must have been: the two of them standing on the freshly scrubbed deck of a Swedish ship, arms around each other, staring beyond the green swell of the Atlantic to the golden hulk of the American continent and the shimmering figure of a promised child. Me. So when I knelt at night to pray, it was their language I whispered, just as Esther had taught me: *Gud som haver barnen kär, Se till mig som liten är*. "God who loves the children, watch over me who is little." Again and again. I did not want to disappoint those who had come so far, and lost so much, to claim me.

Fort Dodge was a promised place for me then, as well. On the weekends, Grandpa and Grandma Price, who lived only a block away, would drive my sisters and me to Dolliver State Park, a few miles downriver, for picnics. We'd wade for hours in Prairie Creek and explore the mossy shadows of Boneyard Hollow, searching for the skulls of bison that had been chased off the sandstone cliffs by Indians. Back home, my mother and I would go for long walks around the yard, stopping at one of her small, semiwild gardens, naming the blossoms and butterflies. And all the birds: the goldfinches at the feeder, the orioles, the iridescent pigeons on Mr. Zimmerman's roof. Neighborhood

children often found their way into our yard, friends with whom
I shared wild adventures in the plum thicket, the bridal hedges,
the muddy space between two garages. Together we turned over
countless rocks, uncovering gobs of swarming, nesting stuff:
ants, ladybugs, snakes. Whole galaxies of life that somehow, until
that moment, had existed beyond sight and care.

 John and Tillie must have known such beauty, I thought.
Esther said that on the weekends, when they were children, her
father would take her and my grandfather for long walks in the
woods along Soldier Creek to fish and pick wildflowers. That
would be in the spring. In the fall, they would collect walnuts
and gooseberries. Always, whatever the season, they'd sit on the
edge of the creek, and John would sing songs to them, one child
on each knee, beneath the hush of the walnut trees and the
oaks. "That place was so beautiful," she'd say. "It should've been
a park." Beautiful, just like my town, my yard. Just like me.

I'm not sure when I stopped believing it. The stories in my
mind just began changing, including those about Haskell
Street. Esther had often told me about the prostitute who had
lived in the house at the northwest corner of the street. One
early evening the poor woman had staggered, naked and sobbing, over to their porch. While John put the kids to bed, Tillie
invited the prostitute into the kitchen for coffee and a blanket.
John sang some stories while the woman blubbered in Norwe-
gian, running her fingers through her red hair. From the bedroom window, Esther watched the woman walk home, their
blanket wrapped around her slender body. This was meant to be
a story about Christian charity, but at some point in early adolescence I began to focus on the nakedness of the woman, on

the improbable fact that one could actually be naked, in the street, for all to see, without caring.

I was in the middle of my own immigrant journey, it seemed. One morning I woke up a foreign place: short, pimply, less than miraculous. Fort Dodge had become alien country as well. It was the 1980s farm crisis in Iowa and people were disappearing. One day a girl would be in class, passing a tightly folded, triangular note, and the next day she'd be gone. "Her family left with the factory," a teacher would say. Another girl, whom I sat with on the band bus, found her recently unemployed father hanging from an electric cord in the garage. Then she disappeared, too. Here was one of the defining stories of our place, the boom-and-bust tragedies of a western agricultural economy, but we didn't study it in our classes. We were given no poverty statistics (nearly 30 percent in some Iowa counties), no depressing demographics, no social or environmental history. We were left to our own devices, which for some meant despair, drugs, and violence. When I wasn't cowering behind my locker door or among my drama buddies, I was the class clown, full of self-deprecation and mimicry, drawing popular caricatures of teachers and submitting cartoons to the school newspaper. And yet at home, on the pages of my private sketchbook, I enacted my own dreams of violence: fist driving into throat, foot into stomach, knife into ribs. Whose throat and stomach and ribs they were changed regularly. Sometimes they were my own.

Around this same time, during a winter escape to Boone, Esther revealed that my great-grandparents had not, in fact, sailed together from Sweden to America. They'd met in Fort Dodge, she said. John had traveled twenty-five days on a cattle boat to avoid the tedium of military service. A decade later, Tillie was apparently seduced into emigrating by a hometown boy who'd left Sweden for Iowa and then returned to recruit for the factories. He'd offered to pay her way, convincing her that they needed skilled seamstresses in America, that she was worthy of his money and his desire, worthy of an entire nation's desire. Then he dumped her.

That night, I lay down on the overstuffed mattress in Esther's guest room and tried to conjure Tillie's arrival in Iowa, reassembling the few details and songs I'd heard, searching for something salvageable as personal myth:

It is April in Fort Dodge—I could picture it—and raining, so the factory smoke hangs low over Central Avenue, smelling like boiled oats and blood. When the driver takes Tillie to the river valley, the mud comes up to the center of the wagon wheels. She has to get out and walk alongside the horses. The man who paid her way is not there to help, and after one look at this place she has lost all desire for him. Another Swedish family takes her in. She picks up dressmaking jobs here and there, but mostly she is a house servant making around four dollars a week. She hates it here. Her only pleasure is to visit a blind friend in Harcourt, another Swedish immigrant woman who hates it here, who refuses to speak English, who touches Tillie's moonish face and sings about the homesick Italian girl who lives in Sweden: *Sa farväl mina drömmar, min barndom sa ljus. Alrig mera jag skada dig fa. Här velle jag leva, här ville jag bo, om inte Italien fanns.* "So farewell my dreams, my childhood so bright. Never more shall I behold you. Here I would want to live, here I would want to settle, if not for Italy." If not for Sweden.

Tillie meets John Anderson—the new story goes—during her first year in Fort Dodge. He is a cooper smith working at Thompson's butter tub factory. He is from Västergötland, which is near Tillie's Småland, so they speak with the same accent. It is enough, in this sorry place, to justify a courtship. John is Evangelical, always talking of heaven, and is eight years older than Tillie is, but she marries him anyway and they settle into the house on Haskell Street. What a mystery he is to her; he is not of this world of mud and shame, her world. Bits of laughter seem always caught in his mustache. Where is he all day that he can emerge covered with sawdust, ashen white, and be an angel of goodwill and song? Wearing loose pants with suspenders— cheekbones like seaside rocks, deep tidal pools for eyes—he walks home from work, so good-natured that maybe two or three dogs follow him, skipping and yelping and begging for his attention.

Soon there is a child, Clara Linea, who tips a kettle of boiling water on herself and dies. She was one year old. A second child, Esther, hates the clunky leather shoes her father makes for her, the ones that cause her ankles to fall inward—not like the satin slippers worn by the rich girls at Bethany Lutheran. A third child, Harold Theodore, is named after the president who waved at Tillie during a whistle-stop in Fort Dodge. Harold, the small shy one who hangs with the wrong crowd and is caught by his father tossing his cap over cigarette butts in the city square, hiding them from the sweeper, so he can deliver them to the older boys in the gang. He is restless, always running off. Tillie dresses Harold like George Washington—that is, like a girl—for the president's birthday celebration at school and won't let him take the short route through the Lord's Prayer. He has to say it all the way through and also, with his father, sing *"Din Port Är Trang,"* the song John will someday request on his deathbed, where he is suffocating from the sawdust in his lungs:

Din port är trang, och smal den stig
Som till Ditt rike bär.
Sa lär mig evangelium, Gud vare därför tack.
Gud vare tack, att även jag far i den staden bo.
Sa lär mig evangelium, Gud Vare därför tack.
Den Langa evighetens dag, i ostörd frid och ro.
I Jesu hjärta, är det rum.

Your door is narrow, and the path is narrow
Which to Your realm leads.
So teach me the gospel, God be praised.
God be praised, that even I may in this City live.
So teach me the gospel, God be praised.
The long day of eternity, in undisturbed peace and quiet.
In the heart of Jesus, there is room.

Fifty years later, a month from high school graduation, it is in this song—escape elevated to divine heights—that I think I've recovered my own story. It is late afternoon in Boone. Aunt Esther has just finished singing *"Din Port Är Trang"* at the piano, and now we are sitting on her enclosed porch, the May sun slipping through the lacy curtains and onto the wood floor. Two easels are set up, one for each of us. I'm painting an alpine meadow, in oils. Esther is painting a desert vista, giving it a mountain, creating dimension with soft cradles of blue that cascade down from peak to foothills. Near the top she adds a wisp

of tangerine, a hint of dusk. Its otherness is godlike. Years earlier, she and Uncle Leonard had planned to move to that desert
landscape, to a retirement village in Green Valley, Arizona, but
then he died. So she sold the property to my grandparents and
they moved there. The immigrant story continues. I'm next to
try to leave, applying to universities on the coasts, but ending
up at the University of Iowa by default, on the other side of the
state. I will fly farther someday, I swear.

Now in my fortieth year, I live in western Iowa in a house near
the Missouri River, just a few hours from Fort Dodge, where my
parents still reside, where my grandparents and great-grandparents
are buried. Esther, too, is at rest in the Boone cemetery. I've
never lived anywhere but Iowa. This has become the unexpected,
defining journey of my life: to come home without ever having
left. When others ask why I've stayed put, I reply with what
must seem the ordinary details of a life: a job, a family, a history. I often mention the place itself: the wildlife and natural areas I've learned to love, the human communities I've called
home, the flawed yet promising terrain that's become as familiar
as my own flesh. All of these answers are true, but none, by
themselves, ever feels complete. Only together, in relation, do
they begin to mean anything. What word is there for this? *Mo-
saic? Ecology? Kinship*—the familial embrace of nature, body,
and spirit.

Whatever it is, I don't think I was fully aware of its tighten-
ing hold on my life, until I traveled for the first time to Haskell
Street over a decade ago. I was in grad school, visiting Fort
Dodge for spring break, and had no particular reason for seeking

it out—just an afternoon drive that suddenly found purpose. Haskell was difficult to locate, but eventually I parked along its short row of boxy, clapboard houses. Behind them rose a steep slope covered with brown foxtail and spots of bald dirt. Across the street was an abandoned industrial park, stubbled with dead grass where the electric plant and creosote tanks used to be. To the east, Haskell ran to a small, undeclared park sporting three gnarled oaks and a runt cedar. To the west, the cracked pavement rose to meet busy Hawkeye Bridge. Beneath that bridge is Soldier Creek, which flows into the Des Moines River, which flows southeast to the Mississippi and on through to the tropical waters of the Gulf and beyond.

I got out of my car and walked to the gray house at 341 Haskell. It was small and unassuming. The porch was now enclosed with dirty aluminum siding, the windows covered with milky plastic, like the eyes of a blind dog. Still, the porch endured, as did the house, and though hard to believe at the time, John had begged to return there to die. That was another story Esther told me. In his sixties, my great-grandfather was diagnosed with TB—more likely white lung from the sawdust—and sent to the sanatorium at Oakdale, now part of the University of Iowa campus. Esther often visited him there, earning her fare by agreeing to comfort those on the bus who were ill or grieving. She and John would sit on his cot, on the screened terrace where the patients slept, even in winter. "Papa looked so sad," she said. "He cried and complained and begged me to take him home." She finally relented and took him back to Haskell, to Tillie, to his chair on the porch.

Esther blamed herself for his death—perhaps at the sanatorium he would've gotten more rest and not walked so much. But every other day John insisted on visiting his son Harold's place to see his infant granddaughter, Sondra, my mother. Kathryn, her mother, would set the baby out on the screened porch and he would look at her from the sidewalk. He didn't want her to get sick. Then he'd walk home alone, visiting the banks of Soldier Creek. When they finally realized John wasn't going to get well, Kathryn brought the baby down to the house on Haskell and let him hold her, just once, for a few minutes, in the chair on the porch. Her body, which would one day give room to my own, had been wrapped in his arms, sheltered and supported by this ground. Here where I was standing.

Strangers live in that house now, and one of them glared at me through the window where Esther had watched the naked prostitute. I stepped across the street to the industrial park. An elevated strip of earth ran along its edge, curving west under the bridge and into the woods. It was probably an old railroad, though the tracks were gone. I followed it toward the woods, letting it move me beneath the bare walnut trees and oaks, their stark branches like veins against the gray March sky. John and his children had often walked in those woods, but I hadn't been there—how perfectly wild and foreign it was. The tall, dry stems of prairie grasses grew near a surprisingly clear Soldier Creek, while black roots stretched from the frozen bank below. White pasqueflowers bloomed on the warm side of the ridge. I sat down and stayed for a long time. Esther was right, it should've been a park.

But it isn't. It's just there, tangled and alive. As I am, still seeking to understand the ways I've been set from the dust. This dust, among these people and creatures, in this place. There is no leaving. There is only the opportunity, as always, to settle, to remember, and be ready. Ready to answer the still insistent demand: *Sjung en visa för os, John!* Sing a story for us!

PART ONE

Departures

THE ROBIN DEFENSE

*P*ut *the baby bird down,* the patrol boy says. *Its momma is coming back and it'll give you lice.*

I tell him I don't care about lice and that I'm going to take the bird to my own momma, but is he in the mood to listen? No. He's in the fifth grade and thinks that wearing a badge and holding a sharp-edged stop sign the size of a pizza dish gives him the power to decide life and death. Another time he might be right, but on this particular spring day, this particular baby bird needs my help—I spotted it in the new wet grass, shivering, on its side, its leg sticking straight out the way they do when things aren't right. Now it's cupped in my hands, a soft, freckled ball, and I think it isn't shivering so much as before.

But is this boy in the mood to listen? He tells me again to put it down and I tell him exactly what I think about patrol boys, what we second-graders call them behind their backs—*the Poop Patrol*—and that he's the stinkiest of them all. Well, that just about does it, he says, and the next thing he has a fistful of my red windbreaker and yanks me backward, but I keep my feet and the bird, and elbow him hard in the breadbasket. He grunts and lets me go, but then his partner, the second stinkiest in the Poop Patrol, grabs hold of my red windbreaker and tells me they're going to send someone to get the principal. That's fine with me, I tell them, because my friend Andy has already gone to get my mother and she'll definitely be on my side. Andy's dad was in the Battle of the Bulge so he'll get her, you can bet on it, even if she's in the bedroom with the door shut, on account of being sad about the funeral. He'll march right up the stairs— he's not afraid of anything, I tell them—and when my mother hears about the bird, she'll come running because she's a nurse and took a sacred oath to heal the sick, which she's done many times before.

But are they in the mood to listen? They just laugh and I say well, OK, *for example,* my mother once healed a freezing, shivering rabbit I found that very winter. It was sitting in my backyard, in a crust of snow, when I walked over and just picked it up with my mittens—it was a very cold day. My mother put it in a box with a blanket and water and some lettuce and the next morning it was gone, hopped away, she said. That's what nurses can do, I tell them, but they just laugh some more and I remind them that if they're not careful the same thing's going to happen to this bird that happened to the albino squirrel—*remember the squirrel?* I think they do, because they stop laughing. They should remember because last fall that white squirrel hung out in the maple tree just across the street, right in front of their faces, and there was a picture of it in the newspaper. They might have even fed it crackers—a lot of kids did since it was almost tame from, well, being fed so many crackers. It came up to me once, close enough to pet, and the newspaper was right, it did have pink eyes. I should've taken that squirrel home to my mother, but we all know the end of that story, don't we?

I think I've struck a nerve, because Pooper Number One pushes me to the ground and the baby bird tumbles from my hands. It lands on its back and just stays there, with the leg pointing a different way, but still not right. I try to pick it up, but Number Two yanks back on the hood of my red windbreaker and that's when I lose it—*Get your paws off me!* I struggle hard, but he has a pretty good grip on my arms by now. I tell them that they both should take a good look at that baby bird, instead of grabbing me all the time. *Don't you see the bugs on its eyes?* They mention the lice and I have to tell them, once again, that I don't care about the lice. *Don't you see that leg sticking out?* But they just keep telling me to leave it be, the momma's coming back, the momma's coming back, even though that isn't true and even if it were, she'd be too late. I'm seven and I know something about babies they don't, that they can die, even when they're just being born, like my brother. *Do you want the baby to die?* I ask them, just in case they read his name in the paper, next to my name, and remember that once they're gone there's no bringing them back, even if it is spring and Easter time and all. You'd think they'd remember that, after the squirrel.

But are they in the mood to listen? They just keep holding my arms and calling me a crybaby—I guess I've started crying—and now the bird is shivering again, in the wet grass, and my mother hasn't arrived yet. What else can I do? What choice have they left me? I relax a little, fake like I've surrendered, then stomp down hard on Number Two's ankle with my big brown shoe. Now he's the one screaming and falling into the wet grass.

I don't wait around for Number One to grab me; I scoop up the bird and dart across the street. They're both standing now, red-faced and thinking about coming after me, thinking about what they might do with that axe-sharp sign of theirs, but then, whatdyaknow, the bell rings.

Too bad, so sad, I tell them, since they're finally listening. *You have to go back to school now and it looks like the principal ain't coming, either!* Number One pulls out his little scratch-and-sniff cheeseburger notebook—I can smell the onions from here—and writes my name in it, but I don't care. I won't be going back to school, ever. Compared to this, school doesn't matter, even though my father says it does and made me go today. Tomorrow's another day, a different story, and I'll have the baby bird to remind him. No. These boys won't see my face again, but I guarantee I'll remember their ugly mugs forever!

That's right, I yell at them, *keep walking! Uh-oh—LOOKEE HERE—I'm carrying the bird with my bare hands, lice and all, and there's nothing you can do!*

They don't turn around, they've stopped listening again, but I don't care. The bird has stopped shivering; he has his shiny black eye on me, because he knows I'm going to take him away and save him. Not like that squirrel. So when the Poop Patrol comes back with the principal, if they come back, they'll have no one to boss except the sun and the air and the mud. Grab them, if you dare, but you won't grab me. I'm gone and so is this baby bird.

I am not a crybaby!

I am in the second grade and don't any of you worry, he'll live, because my mom's a nurse and his name was in the paper and I'll remember. And it's spring.

What Kind of Light?

Our arrival at Camp Mini-Wakan was marked not so much by a sign as by the character of light. In the backseat of the Buick Electra my two younger sisters and I had been asleep, sweaty, open-mouthed, baking in the kind of plastic heat from which I'd awakened during other car trips—usually during the song "Brandy" (she's a fine girl)—and wondered: *Who am I?* But now, as the open fields gave way to the woods, the harsh strike of the sun softened, freckling down through the hackberries and oaks and onto my arms. A cool breeze touched my forehead and drew my face to the window. I saw trees. Lots of trees.

We were going there for Mom, a few months after the baby died—at least, that's how I will always remember it. Mom had spent her childhood summers at Mini-Wakan, a church retreat on the northern Great Lakes of Iowa, and remembered it fondly: the friendships, the horses, the countless Ping-Pong victories. We'd gone there before, as a family, but I didn't expect to return that summer. In April, just after the baby, Mom had seemed to want nothing more than to be away from us, retreating day after day behind the closed door of my parents' bedroom.

A few weeks later, just before our move to the new house, she transformed into a tornado of activity, tossing around boxes, filling them with clothes, toys, blankets, dirty silverware—anything within reach. Watching her, I'd thought the summer already lost. Then, one evening, she appeared at the kitchen table in her flowery nightgown and told Dad that this year she wanted to go somewhere special for her birthday, that there was a spot down by Okoboji Lake where she'd sat alone as a girl and read *My Friend Flicka* all the way through, without stopping. That's where she wanted to go, back to Camp Mini-Wakan. So Dad decided to take her, and us, and you could tell by the way he drove the gravel roads (a little too fast) that he was glad to be going there, too.

Dad parked in front of the log cabin lodge. The air hinted of wood smoke and a thin mist hovered over the nearby meadow, purple with phlox. Inside, while Dad registered, I examined the poster with the cabin assignments. Some cabins had names like Blackfoot and Pawnee and Crow—fierce, noble names—while others had less desirable names like Pocahontas and Sacagawea. I worried that a balsa wood identification tag with a girl's name on it would hold little currency among my friends and would have to be tossed shortly after our return. I finally found our names listed under "Sioux." Dad concurred, it was great luck: Our cabin would be near the lake, not back in the ivy-infested woods like last year or on the smashed-down mud near the latrines.

Carrie Anne, Susan, and I raced to our cabin and through the open doorway. The walls were exposed cedar planks and the floor a dirty cement slab. The smell—pinesap and mildew—

burned my throat, in a good way. Two bunk beds with thin, liver-spotted mattresses were shoved against the walls, and I quickly claimed the top of one of them.

"Sure you want to sleep up there?" Mom asked, throwing her hard white suitcase on the mattress, the suitcase that still contained stray rice from my parents' honeymoon. During our last stay there, I'd rolled off the top bunk and dropped like a meteor. Mom had screamed, snatched me off the concrete, and asked urgent questions: *Do you know your name? Can you count to five?* She'd retrieved Dr. Greenwood, the unofficial camp physician. Nelson Greenwood, who was my age, watched as his father felt my neck and gently rotated my head. Nelson looked disappointed when it was announced that I didn't have a concussion. I know I was. Head injuries were gold.

The Greenwoods were regulars at Mini Wakan. In khaki shorts and tees, toting around their identification guides and Foxfire books, they seemed totally at home in the wild. I admired Dr. and Mrs. Greenwood, and despite Nelson's indifference toward me, they'd always been friendly and generous. Last year, they'd taken Nelson and me to an amusement park across the lake. The rides inside the Fun House were brutal discards from the forties, most of them made of wood. There was the carpet slide and the barrel roll and a whirling, king-of-the-mountain monstrosity called the Sugar Bowl. Dr. Greenwood broke his ankle inside the barrel roll. He'd been shuffling his way through its dark, spinning gut, and the next thing he was on his back, clutching his leg and getting tossed like wet jeans in the dryer. This year Mrs. Greenwood had promised to take us someplace more educational, like the site of the Spirit Lake

Indian Massacre. I looked forward to that, but mostly I looked forward to spending time with Nelson.

Nelson was a genius. In preschool, he could do more with three twigs and a wad of gum than most of us could with a fully loaded tub of Tinker Toys. During those afternoons the other kids and I watched, amazed, as Nelson built gothic castles out of broken chunks of asphalt or used his pocketknife to carve voodoo masks into Mrs. Carroll's bath soap. Then we'd watch him throw a violent tantrum over something like getting the wrong flavor Pixy Stick. He didn't care what anyone thought about him, even grown-ups, and so we hovered around him like moths. Nelson's popularity had only grown. During his frequent battles with our elementary-school teachers, he'd spit out words like *sycophant* and *fascist*. I'd assumed he'd learned these words from his older sisters or from his parents, who, it appeared to me then, had made it their life's ambition never to tell him what to do. Not only had they bought Nelson a microscope, a chemistry set, and a quail egg incubator, but they never required him to keep them or anything else off his bedroom carpet. He'd also been liberated from the humiliation of haircuts. Unlike the rest of us, Nelson was free to walk the earth with shoulder-length hair, his chin in the air as if no one could hurt him or boss him or prove he was wrong. And no one, in my memory, ever had.

At dusk, on our way to the Mini-Wakan lodge for the first campfire, I caught a glimpse of the Greenwoods walking far ahead of us on the trail. There were Nelson and his parents and another boy, limping close beside them. I squinted.

"Who's that crippled boy?"

"We don't point," Mom whispered. "And we don't use the word *crippled*. We use the word *special*."

"Who's that special boy?"

She didn't know. At the outdoor chapel we sat down on one of the log pews. I could see Nelson across the fire, his long hair wavy in the flames. He was shirtless and tan and barefoot, wearing nothing but his olive green shorts with the knife clip (I had a pair myself). He was sitting next to the crippled boy and didn't notice me. Camp Director Jim—tall and sinewy, a mop of curly, sun-yellow hair—called for our attention. He reminded us that every campfire begins with the Johnny Appleseed Prayer, so let's all stand and join in, with feeling:

Oh, the Lord is good to me
And so I thank the Lord
For giving me the things I need,
The sun and the rain and the apple seed.
The Lord is good to me. Amen. Amen-Amen-Amen.

We bent our knees at each *amen*, as if it were a Romper Room exercise and not a prayer.

Jim went over the schedule and the safety rules, and then it was time for games. First, the potato-on-a-spoon relay, in which Dad and Carrie Anne finished dead last. Next, Jim announced the knot-untying contest, and Nelson confidently stepped forward. During school recesses Nelson had impressed us many times with his knot-tying expertise, easily tangling the flag line with sheepshanks and bowlines and cloves. He seemed a sure bet. Jim passed out the knotted pieces of rope and blew his whistle, and the contestants frantically went to work. When

Nelson's first attempt failed, he looked confused, then enraged, bringing the tight jumble down low near his knees as if to break it in half like a stick. His face became a purple bruise. The whistle blew and someone else was declared champion. Jim tried to collect the rope, but Nelson turned away, still yanking at the knot. Finally, he threw it in the dirt and marched to his seat.

Mom covered her mouth to giggle, but I didn't. The reason for Nelson's tantrum—a deep-seated hatred of losing—was the same reason I didn't plan to participate in any game at all. But when Jim announced that the final competition would be a cracker-eating contest, I reconsidered. It would require only the use of my mouth, something at which I was fairly skilled. I stepped forward, and for similar reasons I assumed, so did the crippled boy. Someone cheered, "Yay, Joseph!" We stood next to one another in the line of competitors. I stared at him; he was around my age, the same brown hair, the same summer buzz cut. We looked a lot alike, actually, except he was missing both arms and a leg. In their place were gangly prosthetics, oddly shiny in the firelight. Metallic bolts and wires ran the length of each arm, ending with double hooks that, presumably, could be pinched together. Looking at them I maybe should've felt pity, but mostly I was envious. The kid had hooks.

Jim explained the rules of the contest. It was simple: Our hands would be tied behind our backs and saltine crackers placed in our mouths; a whistle would blow and everyone would start chewing. The first one to whistle would win. Jim tied my hands with rough twine and then, skipping Joseph, did the same to the others. Volunteers came forward from the audience. On Jim's command, a woman wearing a flowered bandana crammed three whole saltines into my mouth. The whistle blew and we began chomping. I realized almost immediately I was in over my head: The salty wafers quickly absorbed all the moisture from my mouth, making it nearly impossible to swallow. Ten seconds in, my jaw was cramping, my tongue straining to dislodge the wet drift of cracker forming against the back of my gums. My head jerked and seized. I glanced at Joseph, who was chewing with a steady, almost elegant rhythm. He appeared poised to win. The crowd roared.

In an all-or-nothing move endemic to poor losers, I tried to whistle too soon. When I puckered and inhaled, several large chunks shot back into my windpipe causing me to cough, delicately at first, then I lunged forward into a screaming hack. Cracker mush flew out of my mouth followed by most of my dinner.

"For godsakes, help him!" my mother screamed.

Jim pounded on my back, nearly knocking me to my knees. Mom charged out of the audience, wrapped her arms around my middle, and gave several quick pulls. I tried to signal her that I was OK, but my hands were tied and my mouth was locked open in dry heave. At last, she put me down and I caught my breath, a wet rope of cracker dangling from my nostrils. The crowd was silent, staring. Even Joseph, cheeks still puffy, had his eyes on me. Nelson was grinning. Desperate to free myself from their faces, I stepped back and did the first thing that came to mind: I whistled.

"He wins!" my mother shouted, hysterical. "He wins!"

Jim looked around, unsure, then handed me the gold-painted medallion. Mom hugged me hard against her hip; there was scattered applause. Jim shakily reviewed the morning schedule, and then everyone walked off toward the cabins, flashlights slicing through the night air.

One of the great things about Camp Mini-Wakan, about the seventies in general, was that parents and children were encouraged, whenever possible, to participate in separate activities. The morning after the cracker contest, while Mom went to find her spot by the lake, I searched alone for Nelson. I discovered him on the steps of his family's cabin, sharpening sticks with a pocket knife. He had stabbed several of them, pointy ends up, into the dirt by the steps. The sticks would scare raccoons and other scavengers away from the cabin door without hurting them, he explained. He said he was against cruelty to animals, and that millions of animals are trapped every year in jagged steel jaws and have to chew their own legs off to escape. I thought of Mom wandering in the woods, unaware.

"What crafts are you going to make?" I asked. Last year I'd made a macaroni cross, a beaded bracelet, and a lanyard with a key clip at the end of it. This year, I hoped to graduate to leather wallets decorated with rattlesnakes and horses, just like the ones my dad's law clients sent him from prison. Nelson said he wasn't going to make any crafts; he was going to search for something in the woods.

"For what?"

"Just something."

Nelson folded his knife, stood up, and began walking down the trail. I paused, waiting for an invitation, then fell in behind. As I entered the woods the chill air closed around me, but Nelson's pace was brisk and I soon warmed. We didn't talk, so the cries of birds, the tussle of leaves seemed to amplify, as if we weren't walking on the earth but up high among them. We stepped single file until Nelson veered off the trail. I hesitated at the edge of the undergrowth—it looked thick and dark—then plunged in, my socks getting soaked with dew as I struggled to keep up. I followed him around a slippery hill to a clearing where the trees were spaced wide and the sun threw spots on the green. Nelson stopped to examine a rotten piece of bark and, nearby, a delicate shelf of mushrooms. I stood back, wondering, but he was beyond me in that moment, so full of purpose that it made me feel empty. To me the place was a mass of indistinct life, but to him it was a seer's palm, to be touched and read. I looked for something I might recognize, finding only a small patch of horsetail reeds. I picked one strand, then another, disassembling their squeaky joints until Nelson was ready to move on.

I had my suspicions about Nelson's search—his leopard salamander had recently died and been dissected, so he would need a new one. Those suspicions seemed to be confirmed when we arrived at the marsh. It covered a large opening in the woods, dense with cattails and algae and the grind of frogs, smelling like old rainwater in a garbage can. Nelson walked the edges, ankle deep, peering into the shallows. Slowly, he moved out toward the cattails, where the dank water reached above his waist. I kicked off my sneakers and followed. The water was warm, the mud soft. I waded out a little farther then stopped. Nelson was on the edge of the rushes, water up to his chest, when he finally turned to look at me. He waved his arm, signaling me to join him, but I stood in place. He waved again. I stepped back toward the shore.

At a nearby tree, I crouched down and tried to look as if I was searching for something. For my birthday, Nelson's mom had given me a series of picture books on natural habitats, from which I'd learned that marshes and swamps were home to a large mix of life, most of it unpleasant. There were your basic tadpoles and bullfrogs and dragonflies, but just beneath the surface, in any given spot, there might also be leeches and water snakes and snapping turtles. *Alligator* snapping turtles, to be precise. My younger cousin, Dave, and I had traced their monstrous, prehistoric portraits from that book: the deformed, punched-up faces, the black eyes, the six-foot-long jagged bodies stuffed into grotesquely undersized shells. The pictures appeared to confirm the legends we'd been told, how they could take off fingers in one bite and how if they clamped onto you they wouldn't let go until sundown, even if you cut their heads off. Dave and I had coauthored an illustrated novel on the subject. When we showed it to our grandfather Roy, he shared his own story about a boy he'd known in Missouri who'd been dragged by a snapper to the bottom of a catfish pond. Nothing left of him but bits.

So, I'd retreated to shore, which I could've blamed entirely on the turtles except that during the previous summer—despite the nature books and Grandpa's stories—I'd fearlessly waded, hip deep, in the marsh at Dolliver Park and the duck pond at Northlawn Cemetery. From there to here, something had changed in me. I'd first noticed it on a picnic at Dolliver with Grandpa Roy earlier that spring. Instead of splashing in Prairie

Creek with my sisters as usual, I'd found myself watching them from the bank, bewildered by fear. I'd still walked the trails that day and climbed rocks, but I'd become suspicious of surfaces— water, algae, even tall grass—hesitant to break them, as if there might be something lurking there, waiting.

"What are you looking for?"

Nelson was beside me, his wet clothes freckled with pond scum.

"Bloodroot," I said, pulling from memory one of the few plant names I knew.

"Here it is, right in front of your face." He pinched the stem off a broad leaf plant and sure enough, it bled. He ran it the length of his forearm, like a knife wound.

"Why did you get out of the water?" he asked. "Were you afraid?" I told him I had things to look for in the woods. He asked me why I was afraid. I said I wasn't afraid, and when he asked again, I did what he always did when losing an argument: I changed the subject.

"So how do you know Joseph?"

Nelson picked another bloodroot to scar his cheeks and told me Joseph was from Keokuk and that his parents had met him at a church conference and invited him to go to camp with them.

"That's too bad about his arms," I said.

"Why's it too bad?"

"Well, he doesn't have any."

"And why do you suppose that is?"

I stood up to answer—the words were right there, lifted by the voices of my grandmother Kathryn and other grown-ups, overheard in prayer: *God's will be done*. Any other summer, wading fearlessly in the Dolliver marsh, that's exactly how I might have responded: *God's will*. But now the words were stuck.

"Because . . . God . . . "

Nelson's arms flew into the air.

"That's stupid! How do you even know God is real? My sister Kenna says that if there's a God, he'd stop bad things from happening like war and people starving. And anyway, Joseph got that way because his mom took some medicine while she was pregnant. There're lots of kids like him; he's not the only one."

I'd tried to talk with Nelson about God before, but he'd just ignored me, acting annoyed. Mom had said that unlike Grandma Kathryn some people prefer not to talk about God, even though they believe. I'd assumed Nelson was one of those people. Now I felt small and exposed and more than anything just wanted him to go away. I turned my back and pretended to look for more bloodroot.

"I'm going in the water," he said. "There's a bunch of blue herons on the other side of the cattails. I saw them, but you won't. You're scared."

I slowly moved away from the marsh until I found the thin line of our footsteps through the undergrowth. I let it draw me beneath the trees and back to camp.

I didn't see Nelson the rest of the day or at campfire. The next morning he showed up, still shirtless and barefoot, at the dock with his parents and Joseph. I stepped behind Mom, out of view. We were all waiting to canoe to the site of the Spirit Lake

Indian Massacre. My sisters had thought it sounded scary and opted to spend the day crafting. Mom was upbeat—as a girl, she'd often canoed on the Lakes—and so was Dad. He'd been a history major at Iowa Teachers and wanted to see the location of what his professor had called "the saddest event in the whole of Iowa history." I was there because Grandpa Roy had stoked me with talk of decapitations and scalps and the possibility of finding arrowheads. But now, as I gazed across the vast surface of the lake, I felt the fear rise in me like dough.

After inspecting our candy-striped life preservers, Jim ran through the basics of canoeing: The person in back steers, the person in front paddles, and the person in the middle just sits there for stability. Dad immediately moved to the back, leaving Mom in front to paddle and me in the middle. I watched the Greenwoods glide their canoe smoothly from sand to water. Nelson sat in the front, working his large paddle with surprising grace. When it came our turn to launch, Dad threw his entire body against the canoe and had to leap to avoid getting wet, which caused the canoe to lurch violently. Mom screamed and I grabbed onto the sides, revealing to everyone the depth of our wilderness skills. After Dad settled into his seat, my parents began the process of coordinating their paddle strokes, which, like coordinating their personalities, proved difficult. While the others stayed near the shore, we were zigzagging out to sea.

"Keep it left, Sondra! Left!"

"Aye aye, Captain!"

I was a wreck inside, afraid my parents' bickering might cause the canoe to capsize, throwing me into the water, into the jaws of whatever was surely waiting there. To Jim, though, I must have appeared to be the only one in the canoe doing my job. Hands on the sides, white-knuckled, I was the rock of stability.

Mom and Dad eventually got the hang of the canoe, which began moving in a sort of straight line, closer to shore. Mom recited the names of a surprising number of birds and trees that she remembered from her days at camp. She recounted what she'd learned about the natural history of the lakes, how they'd been created by an ancient mile-thick glacier that had once covered the region. Hands still locked on the sides, I tried to see our surroundings through her eyes, as a kind of long campfire story. A story that might contain prehistoric beasts and, equally fantastic, my mother as a girl my own age. And also the God she and Grandma had taught me to believe in, holding, as her favorite camp song went, the whole world in his hands. Including me. Including the lake, which, right then, I wanted very badly to touch. I reached out my hand—How cold, how deep might the water be?—and quickly removed it.

Dad beached the canoe as successfully as he'd launched it. Shoes squishing, we joined the rest of the group standing in a large, well-groomed clearing. There was a log cabin surrounded by marigolds and a tall, needle-shaped monument. Our guide, a bearded, thick old man wearing shorts with suspenders, called us over. He said his name was Arthur and that he was happy to be visiting with us about one of the most famous and horrible events in the history of the Iowa frontier: the Spirit Lake Indian Massacre. The massacre began, he said, on a bright March morning in 1857, just as the Gardner family was settling down for Sunday breakfast in that cabin right there behind us. At the table were Mr. and Mrs. Gardner; their daughter Abbie, who was thirteen, and their son, Rowland, who was six. Their eldest daughter was also there with her husband and his buddy. A regular family get-together. Suddenly, the meal was interrupted by a Sioux warrior standing in the doorway. The warrior asked for food and was invited to join the family at the table. Soon more Indians arrived, demanding more food and also ammunition, which the friendly, unsuspecting Gardners supplied.

"But this was not just your run-of-the-mill gang of savages," Arthur declared, eyebrows raised. Led by the ruthless Inkpaduta, this bunch had been robbing and harassing white settlers up and down the Little Sioux River all winter. The Gardners were far out of reach of civilization, so they hadn't heard of Inkpaduta's sinister activities. After the Indians stole the family's cattle, the two young men at the cabin left to warn other families. They were promptly killed and scalped. The Indians returned, demanding more food, and when Mr. Gardner reached to get it, they shot him in the back. The women tried to interfere—Arthur raised his arms in the air—but they were dragged outside and beaten to death with gun stocks right about where we were standing. The boy had his brains bashed out against an oak tree. Abbie, the thirteen-year-old, was taken hostage and toted along to other pioneer cabins, where she witnessed more bloody and decapitated bodies, some of them the bodies of children. By the time it was over, thirty-two people were dead. Abbie was one of the few survivors and would later return to this site, purchase the cabin, and sell frontier souvenirs and copies of her eyewitness account, which, Arthur reminded us, were still available for purchase.

"The worst of it," he concluded, "is that none of these savage murderers were ever brought to justice."

Arthur said he'd be happy to answer any questions, but we just stood there, staring into our imaginations like bystanders at a car wreck. I kept thinking about that little boy. What was it like for him before he died, being swung round and round through the air, the leaves and sky bleeding into each other? Did he know what was about to happen to him? Did he fight it? Or did he extend his arms into the breeze as if he were only in the playful grip of his father—confusing (as I knew could happen) one thing for another, death for life? I looked around at the various tree trunks, searching for a stain or thin spot or even the faint imprint of a face.

As our group gradually dispersed, I spotted Nelson zipping toward Arthur.

"You got it wrong," he said.

"What?"

"You got it wrong. You left stuff out."

Most of the crowd, including my parents, had moved on to the cabin, but several remained to watch the developing skirmish. I tucked in behind them. Arthur put his hands in his pockets, looked down at Nelson, and smiled.

"What stuff might that be, young man?"

"You didn't say how those Sioux were starving to death and how their families had been shot and how they'd had their land stolen and how white people gave them diseases. You didn't talk about any of *those* things."

Arthur winked at some of the parents, as if to say, "This one's watched a little too much public television."

Many years later, in graduate school, long after Nelson and most of my childhood friends had disappeared from my life, I'd learn more about the chain of events leading to the massacre. It probably began when Henry Lott, a white horse thief, murdered a Sioux leader named Two Fingers and his entire family. A coroner's jury in Homer, Iowa—a small, nearly abandoned town I'd often seen from the road—blamed Henry Lott for the murders, but he was never arrested. Instead, the decapitated head of Two Fingers ended up dangling from a pole in downtown Homer, his double rows of teeth drawing crowds for days. Some claimed that Inkpaduta was a relative of Two Fingers, and that he might have slaughtered the Spirit Lake settlers out of revenge. But there were other possibilities: the smallpox that scarred Inkpaduta's face, the fact that the Gardners were squatting on Sioux land, the hard prairie winter that had left many Indians weak and starving, fighting with crows for waste corn. While reading all this in an isolated carrel at the university library, I would think of Nelson and wonder, as always, how he'd known such things. How it was that among all those educated adults, his voice had been the only echo of the larger story.

"You're right," Arthur said, leaning down so he was close to Nelson's face, "but, young man, that's no excuse for killing people the way they did. That's no excuse." He turned and started to walk away, but Nelson kept after him.

"Why not? Why isn't it OK to kill people who are trying to kill you? Or if your kids are starving to death, why isn't it OK to kill to get some food?"

"It just isn't," Arthur said, veering like a buzzard harassed by a redwing.

"Oh, yeah?" Nelson said, face burning. "Well, I hope someday your kids starve!"

A woman stepped in—Was it his mother?—and held Nelson's arm, preventing him from pursuing Arthur any farther.
She crouched and said something to him that I couldn't hear.
"But he's wrong!" he kept saying. "You know he's wrong!" She
nodded, but then she said something that made Nelson burst
into tears. He broke loose and ran off toward the beach. A few
people watched him disappear and shook their heads.

I didn't see Nelson much during the rest of the week. There he'd
be at breakfast or at evening campfire and then, a moment later,
he'd be gone. I tried not to miss him. I filled my days with crafts
and with new friends, like Joseph. After Joseph won the medal for
catching the biggest fish, I congratulated him, perhaps hoping to
make up for the cracker-eating debacle. We talked a lot after that.
Joseph was the first crippled person I'd ever known and I studied
him closely. There was nothing he seemed unable to do. At dinner I watched him use his hooks to lift the fork and spoon and, at
craft tables, tie yarn around Popsicle sticks. On nature hikes I
watched him pick flowers and climb rocks. I even watched him
steer a sailboat. It was no surprise, then, near the end of the week,
to see him in line with the rest of us for horseback riding.

The camp horses were a mix of size and disposition, and I
recognized some of them from our previous visit. There was
Chocolate, the old quarter horse—he was the biggest but also
the slowest, refusing to gallop across the final stretch of
meadow. He was one to avoid. Junior, the small paint, was another undesirable—you'd spend the whole ride looking up an-

other horse's crack. Romeo, the most handsome with his gold coat and jet-black mane, was reserved for Jim. I ended up with Rose, a red Appaloosa who, though gassy, could really break it open across the flats. I felt lucky. Mom and Carrie Anne, the only ones there from my family, would be riding together on Chocolate. They'd be pulling up the rear, for sure.

Joseph was assigned Dusty, another Appaloosa, and I watched as he placed his good leg in the stirrup and swung the other over her back like a pro. He sat tall and easy in the saddle as we ambled onto the trail. I trotted up alongside and asked if he'd ridden before. He said that it was one of his favorite things to do, along with board games, which he described at length. I gathered my courage. I'd never asked Joseph why he was the way he was, but now that camp was ending, it seemed my most urgent mission. Nelson, back at the marsh, had provided the scientific explanation, but I was looking for something else, an answer to the question still growing inside me: *How do you even know God is real?* I would've asked my parents, but they hadn't mentioned God much recently, which made me think they were tender about it, that my question might hurt them, which was the last thing I wanted to do. Then it occurred to me, as I watched Joseph participate in all the activities and then at dinner cross his hooks in prayer, that he might know something about the subject. This could be my last chance to find out.

"So, how come you don't have any arms?"

Joseph looked kindly at me from the back of his horse, as if he'd been asked this question before. He repeated what Nelson had told me, that his mother had taken pills—thalidomide—and that he'd been born that way.

"Does it bother you?"

"Not really. I've always been this way, so I'm used to it."

He didn't get my point. "I mean, does it ever bother you that you're this way? You know, does it *bother* you?"

"You mean, am I angry? Yeah, sometimes, but not very much. It was an accident and God helps me to do a lot of things. He made me this way for a reason, I guess."

The conversation moved on, but inside the sweet relief flowed. There *is* a God, and he acts with goodness and reason— Joseph had said so, and who would know better than this boy with no arms who'd spent the last week fishing and hiking and sailing and right now, here beside me, riding a horse? Nelson had been wrong, and the more I thought about it, the angrier I became. As Rose trotted across the upland prairies, the tall grass scratching my ankles, I pictured the moment when I'd confront Nelson with his own stupidity, shame him, as he'd done to me back at the marsh.

Mom and Carrie Anne shouted for me to slow down— Chocolate, as predicted, was lagging behind. I told Joseph I'd see him later. Before Chocolate could catch up, Rose, along with most of the other horses, broke into a gallop, anticipating home. "Hang on!" Mom shouted, but I wasn't worried; I felt snug inside the stirrups, rocking smoothly with the horse's body, the wind clearing the water from my eyes. Up ahead, though, I could see that the brush-lined trail was too narrow for the horses to pass one another, and that they were jamming together. A few of the horses, including Joseph's, veered off into the pasture. Joseph bounced in the saddle as Dusty tore over the rough terrain toward a group of trees. The first couple of riders ducked, clearing the low branches, but for some reason Joseph didn't duck. He raised his arms, and when Dusty passed beneath, they smacked against the branch, sliding him back out of the saddle. I expected to see him fall, but he just dangled there, swinging, his hooks embedded in the branch.

"Help me!" he screamed.

I pulled hard on the reins, stopping Rose, and shouted for Jim. When he saw Joseph, he charged over and positioned his horse, Romeo, beneath the branch. Joseph settled safely into the front of the saddle, but Jim was having trouble dislodging the hooks. He yanked at them for a while, then paused to study the situation. Finally, he lifted Joseph's shirt, revealing a plastic shell and a series of belts and straps that, one by one, he carefully unhitched. Romeo eased forward and Joseph slipped free. For the first time I saw his stumps—they looked pinched-off and tender. Joseph sobbed as they rode by, Jim's long arms wrapped around him as if he was a helpless baby.

"He's going to be OK." I hadn't heard Mom ride up beside me. "He's not hurt; he's just scared. We'd better keep going."

I held my horse in place and stared at Joseph's arms, still gripping the branch, their straps dangling like piñata ribbons.

That night we gathered for the final campfire. Everyone sang— *The Lord said to Noah, "There's gonna be a floody floody"*—and clapped and stomped their feet, including Joseph, who appeared to have fully recovered his confidence as well as his arms. He stood between Dr. and Mrs. Greenwood, smiling, as if nothing unusual had happened that day. He kept on smiling through the counselor skits—about "the big one that got away" and another about a clownish Indian war dance (the actors wore ferns in their hair) in which one Indian couldn't find his rhythm. The confused brave stuttered and shuffled and threw down his tomahawk in humorous disgust. Almost everyone laughed, but I didn't. I looked around for Nelson. There was something in me that longed to hear his defiant voice.

The camp minister eventually called on us to make a circle around the fire, hold hands, and sing, one more time, the Johnny Appleseed song. Then he asked us to bow our heads in silent prayer and recall, as Johnny had, the many gifts God had given us that week: friendship, laughter, communion with nature. The group fell silent, but I kept my eyes open. Next to me, Mom and Dad were holding hands, eyes shut tight. Mom's cheeks were wet. Soon we'd be moving into the new house, the one with the big yard and the extra bedroom none of us would use—not until a year or so later, when another baby, Allyson, would be born. By then, the happy Mom we knew would return, but not the entirety of my earlier faith. I think I sensed it even then, staring through the flames at Joseph. His hooks were crossed, his head bowed, but I knew better. Joseph could do all the praying he wanted and talk about how God had helped him, but his horse would still charge under that tree and snag him like a kite. His arms would still be unstrapped from his body—because he didn't have any arms—and left hanging from the branch. I couldn't scare that image out of my mind, those arms, that vulnerability. Nor the sense of all our lives drifting up, like sparks from the fire, toward an empty sky.

The prayer ended and there was more singing and clapping. As I lined up for s'mores, I felt a poke in the ribs. I turned and saw Nelson, wide-eyed and dirty, standing at the edge of the firelight. He'd come back for me. I dropped my plate and ran after him, catching up just inside the woods. "I've got something to show you," he whispered, and disappeared into the darkness. This time I didn't hesitate to follow.

I couldn't see anything. At first I was unsure of myself, stepping carefully, flailing my arms. But when nothing happened— no stumbling, no sticks in the eye—I settled into an unfamiliar trust. Vision became a matter for other senses to decide: the sound of Nelson's footsteps, the smell of a nearby pine, the touch of leaves. I walked steadily, inside my breathing, inside a place beyond thought, until, I don't know how long, I heard Nelson stop.

"Up here," he said. I felt the earth rise beneath me: a steep bank. I put my hands on it, cool, rough with sticks and needles and the damp edges of leaves. I crawled until I bumped into Nelson's legs. "Look," he said. I stood up. Out there, floating like ghosts, were dozens of bluish white lights.

"What are they?" I gasped.

"Fungus—I've been looking for it all week. Come see."

I followed him to one of the lights and saw that it wasn't floating; it was nestled against the base of a tree. Nelson lifted one of the bright embers.

"Are you scared?" he asked.

"No."

He grinned and placed it in my hand. I expected it to feel hot against my skin, but it was cool, a chunk of dead mossy bark. I ran my finger across the velvet surface and stared into the glow. What kind of light is it, I wondered, that never has to be switched on, that never burns? I looked at Nelson. What kind of light?

MOLE MAN LIVES!

⬛━╳━⬛

Between my eighth and fourteenth year I grew approximately six inches. Which is to say, not at all. There is never a good time to be a short boy in America, but the late seventies and early eighties were especially challenging. The Randy Newman song "Short People (Got No Reason to Live)" was immensely popular, as were Troll Dolls and Gnomes. Gary Coleman ruled. Then there was my own sister, Carrie Anne, who was two years younger than me, but who'd had the audacity to grow two inches taller—the rogue cornstalk towering above the bean plant. That's how it felt sometimes, and there were moments when I would've appreciated someone ripping her out of my life by the roots just to be rid of the comparison. And the danger. Almost the very instant my sister stepped into the hallways of Fort Dodge North Junior High School, she commenced telling the most monstrous bullies that her "big brother" was going to pound them straight.

"Carrie Price?" I'd say as one after another of these bullies shoved me against the lockers. "Never heard of her!"

In retrospect, I should've appreciated Carrie Anne's confidence, since she was about the only girl at North to take me seriously. My popularity in elementary school, where everyone was pretty much the same size, had set me up for a hard fall in this regard. I'd even had a girlfriend in the sixth grade, with whom I'd logged many miles, hand in hand, around the sparkling perimeter of Carousel Roller Rink. I'd given her a gold-plated "promise" ring with my initial *J* engraved into it, which she gave back to me just before the big move to junior high. Our parting was amicable, both of us deciding that we needed to play the field. I took this responsibility seriously and, upon arriving at North, carefully observed a number of candidates, weighing their qualifications as potential soul mates. When I finally offered my ring to a ninth-grade cheerleader, she looked down at me in horror.

"What's the *J* stand for? Jellybean?"

I tried to remain positive. That spring, and every junior high spring thereafter, I handed my yearbook to the most beautiful girls at North, girls for whom I would've gladly thrown myself on a spit, hoping they'd write something suggestive or just encouraging. Instead, they wrote things like "To a cute little kid with lots of smarts. Best of luck in the future!" and "To a super sweet guy! Keep up the artwork!" and "To a good buddy who makes me laugh! Don't ever change!"

Translation: *Go Kill Yourself.*

Short boys, like stellar white dwarves, tend to collapse in on themselves, imploding toward clinical depression, drugs, and Dungeons and Dragons, to name just a few possibilities. Any one of these might have been my fate, if it hadn't been for my cocker spaniel puppy, Bilbo Baggins. He needed walking, which meant I had to leave the solitary dangers of my bedroom and jog him around the neighborhood or into the "North Woods"—a couple of forested acres bordering the nearby football stadium. We visited the woods often enough that I built a small shelter there with fallen branches and discarded sheet metal gathered along the tire-choked drainage creek. It even included a chicken-wire addition for Bilbo, whose wild spirit required the occasional containment. Together, we lost whole afternoons out there, listening to the black swarms of starlings and grackles, eating fistfuls of mulberries and plums, observing the searching, intelligent behaviors of wood roaches and rats. In certain light, new worlds were revealed: hidden pools and rainbows of fungus and fantastic colonies of mushrooms that have yet to be identified by science. There was a giant woodchuck who, like a pagan god, would sometimes emerge from the earth and shock the whole place into reverent silence. There were grander natural places in the Fort Dodge area, such as Brushy Creek and Dolliver State Park, where my family picnicked on the weekends, but I considered the North Woods a personal gift: the one place within walking distance where I was neither tall nor short, and where solitude was a kind of freedom.

Unfortunately, that still left a few hours in the day to hang out alone in my room, doing the white dwarf thing. For me, it was comic book art. As several otherwise uninterested girls noted in my yearbook, I was good with a pencil. I filled entire sketchbooks with the elaborate adventures of my own pint-sized, nature-fused superheroes: Crab Boy, Mosquito, and The Amazing Blue Mud Dauber. They battled a festering hive of supervillains—among them Deltoid, Handsome Horribilus, and The Sportster—who bore a remarkable resemblance to the taller, more popular boys at school. In my stories, the short guy always got the girl. As the bitter fissure between fantasy and reality widened, however, I increasingly identified with the villains I read about in my Marvel comic books. Especially the deformed souls who'd once been good, but due to the cruelty of others or a poorly planned science experiment, had been transformed into revenge-obsessed monsters. Several of the Marvel villians took on the identities of unpopular animals and insects, such as Lizard, Scorpion, and the Vulture. Creatures who, like others I knew, had been unjustly oppressed due to size, looks, and/or disposition.

My favorite was Mole Man, the first official foe of the Fantastic Four—the "strangest menace of all time!" His story, as I first encountered it in a Marvel anthology, began with the Fantastic Four investigating immense holes that had appeared all over the globe, out of which giant monsters were emerging and wreaking havoc. The heroes eventually traced the source to Monster Isle, where, far beneath the surface, they confronted the diabolical mastermind—Mole Man! Short, pockmarked, sporting nerdy blue glasses, a green jumpsuit, and a wrinkled cape, Mole Man shared with them his sad story: "It all started long ago!! Because the people of the surface world mocked me!" In the next frame, his memory, there is an attractive woman with a disgusted look on her face: "What? ME go out with YOU? Don't make me laugh!" In the next, a sharp-dressed, serious entrepreneur: "I KNOW you're qualified, but you can't work here! You'd scare our other employees away!" In the next, a dapper gent adjusting his tie in the men's room mirror: "Hey, is that your face, or are you wearin' a *MASK! HAW HAW!*" In his despair, the tormented pariah escaped across vast seas and polar ice caps, because, as he put it, "Even this loneliness is better than the cruelty of my fellow men!" On Monster Isle, he accidentally stumbled down a cavernous hole, falling to the center of the earth, blinded and stranded—"like a human mole!" Soon, however, he mastered the native gargoyles, built an underground empire, and began plotting his conquest of the surface world. Unlike me, the Fantastic Four were unmoved by Mole Man's story and, following a prolonged battle, blew up Monster Isle, dooming him to a fiery death.

"It's best that way!" Mr. Fantastic exclaimed as they fled in their nuclear space jet. "There was no place for him in our world . . . perhaps he'll find peace down there   "

I was surprised by how deeply I grieved Mole Man's death. His anger, though misdirected, seemed justified: The real fault was with a people whose indifference and cruelty had created the very "monsters" they later congratulated themselves on destroying. Why couldn't the Fantastic Four see that they were merely pawns of that society, its eager thugs, so busy fighting the symptoms of evil they had no time to investigate the causes? *Heroes?* More like assassins.

A little later, while perusing another Marvel anthology, I was relieved to discover that Mole Man had actually survived the destruction of Monster Isle. At the last second he'd escaped through a tunnel dug by his blindly obedient gargoyles, rebuilt his Subterranea Empire off the coast of New Jersey, and constructed retractable platforms under major cities in the U.S. and

Russia in the hopes of provoking nuclear Armageddon. The Fantastic Four discovered his plot, but this time appeared to be too late. "When next I appear on the surface," Mole Man proclaimed as he pushed the Doomsday button, "all of earth shall be MINE!" Unbeknownst to him, and me, Mr. Fantastic had rearranged the wiring so nothing sank beneath the surface except Mole Man's isle itself. Once again, there was no attempt to save or reform him. As the heroes flew off in their jet, the Thing quipped, "Ol' boss man fixed it so that Shorty blew his OWN little island right off the map!"

Shorty—that was enough in itself to cement the bond between us. Little did they know, however, that Mole Man had once again avoided oblivion, this time escaping through the subterranean tunnels of my unconscious mind, entering the mythic baseline of adolescence. There he waited, as always, to resurface and be avenged.

⚬⚬⚬⭤⚬⚬⚬

The dawn of my sophomore year, the first at the high school, seemed promising. I'd enjoyed a modest growth spurt over the summer, finally surpassing Carrie Anne. Five foot and almost two inches. This was uncharted territory for me—the forest of five-footers—and I was confident my romantic fortunes would improve, now that I could look a girl or two in the nostrils. But the ladies did not flock to my still unimpressive perch. Neither did popularity or fame. The number of my good friends remained the same (six, including my mother), but I soon lost several to the intellectually glamorous debate team, Nelson Greenwood among them. There they assumed their rightful stature alongside future lawyers, civic leaders, and other fortunates who had tongue-kissed and thus had reason to care about this state of misery known as civilization.

In contrast, I drifted toward extracurriculars that encouraged self-delusion and escapism, such as band, Latin Club, and drama. I discovered early on, however, that the French horn offered little chance for future glory and that Latin was dead. So I threw myself into acting, one of the few professions where it appeared short men could receive the wealth and adoration they'd so painfully earned. Some of our most glamorous male leads— Robert Redford, Tom Cruise, Arnold Schwarzenegger—were shorter than they appeared on screen. By focusing on their Hollywood successes, I was able to ignore the more sobering examples, such as Paul Williams and Hervé Villechaize (aka Tattoo). Paul Williams was a brilliant songwriter and very short, but like me, not particularly handsome. Consequently, he was given such primo roles as beer smuggler "Little" Enos Burdette in *Smokey and the Bandit* and a pedantic orangutan in the final, pathetic installment of the *Planet of the Apes* movies. In contrast, Kris Kristofferson, also a brilliant songwriter, but tall and handsome, got to bang Sarah Miles in *The Sailor Who Fell from Grace with the Sea*. Williams and Kristofferson actually crossed paths in *A Star Is Born*. Paul gave Barbara Streisand the hit song for the movie ("Evergreen"), while Kris, as usual, gave her the business.

Fate wasn't as kind to Hervé Villechaize. A few years after he left *Fantasy Island,* he killed himself.

In the fall of sophomore year, I successfully auditioned for a part in the school play, *One Foot in Heaven.* This drama was actually set in Fort Dodge, based on a true story, and had been turned into a movie starring Henry Fonda. It portrayed the trials and tribulations of Reverend Spence as he attempts to inspire his "unique" congregation to build a new Methodist church—the very church where my parents had been married. I was cast as spoiled and precocious Georgie, boy-son of Mrs. Digby, a choir singer. I wore tight knickers and a chauffeur's cap, and my best line was "Aw, Mom!" after which I jumped into my stage mother's arms. She had no trouble holding me. The yearbook called it a "humorous, touching story," and I was singled out in the paper for an especially entertaining performance. I followed this with a successful spring run as Freckles in *The Perils of Priscilla.* In this classic melodrama, I helped dimwitted hero Harlowe Starbuck foil the dastardly plans of mustache-twiddling Smedley Smidgin to close the country school and deflower our teacher, Miss Priscilla. After the final performance, a couple of second-graders asked for my autograph.

These accolades were intoxicating, but unfortunately (and at the time, unbelievably) they didn't earn me any romantic entanglements. Many of the girls in drama were beautiful and smart, but as I told my male colleagues, they were too willing to compromise those gifts for the attention of the stupid and the popular. Here was necessity disguised as principle. In truth, I would have compromised almost anything if I thought it would make a difference—we all would have—and this larger fiction was the glue that cemented our friendship. We were all, in a sense, veterans of the same *tableau vivant,* its stage encapsulating the entire school, the town, and surrounding countryside, which during the farm crisis seemed to be wilting before our eyes. Onto that stage we'd been cruelly tossed to endure our assigned roles until the final, merciful curtain. Among these boys I discovered an unspoken understanding that encouraged the kind of vicious fantasies I'd until then indulged in secret. I allied myself with upperclassmen like Chaz Willingham and Daniel Baker, whose extended tour had made them gifted cynics, especially quick with the sarcasm, but also generous and kind to those of us just joining the show. It felt as if I'd wandered for a long time and finally found refuge—not among trees and fungus, but at last among fellow human beings.

At the end of the year, my fellow actors honored me with the Golden Brick Award (literally, a gold-painted brick) for Outstanding Sophomore Actor, setting the bar even higher for my junior career. I sustained another growth spurt over the summer—five foot four!—which meant that, theoretically, I could play adult roles. While auditioning for the fall play, *Mr. Hobbs' Vacation,* I salivated over the lead, but was cast instead as a rheumatic old barber, Sidney Bollivar, whom I initially played with a Dixie drawl and a limp. I was attempting to lend the character some depth, to hint at unacknowledged tragedies, both personal and historical, but the effect was lost on our director. Mr. Beck had enjoyed an award-winning career as a high school drama coach, sending several students on to fame in community theaters around the nation. This was the tail end of that career and it was a harsh one. During rehearsals, Mr. Beck sat in the dark margins of the auditorium, smoking cigarettes, crossing and uncrossing his thin, Ichabod legs. The loathing hovered, along with the smoke, in a gray cloud above his head. During my one scene, he'd occasionally yell out and charge the stage: "No, No, NO! Don't cross in front of the main actor and for godsake stop limping around and talking like a cracker—if you review the script, you'll notice there's no part for a polio victim from Tupelo! You're in Maine, boy, *MAINE!*"

The play was successful, attendance brisk, but then, during the final performance, I forgot a line—an important line. Thanks to Chaz's improvisation, no one in the audience noticed my mistake, but Mr. Beck did. Afterward, he threatened, through gasps of smoke, to cut me from Drama Club if I didn't stop "messing around." How could I explain to him that I hadn't been messing around? That I was more serious about acting than I was about almost anything else in my life? I'd obsessively practiced those lines and knew them perfectly, and yet somehow my body—my brain—had betrayed me. I worried it might be related to my new pimple medication. Cystic acne had blossomed all over my face like a ripe poppy field. This was a potentially lifelong condition and I found myself begging doctors for a miracle cure. A dermatologist eventually prescribed an experimental acne medication, but he was disconcertingly vague about the possible side effects—sterility, depression, memory loss, a third arm growing out of my head . . . Who knew? One thing was clear, though: short of a skin graft, there were no other options.

Whatever caused me to forget that line, I decided it would be best for everyone involved if I returned full time to what I did best: sitting alone in my room, counting zits, and talking to my dog. I came from a loving family, but there are times in the history of the body when one's condition cannot be fully appreciated by another human being. This was one of those times and I instinctively turned to Bilbo, entrusting him with my emotional life because he appeared to be the only one up to the task. That is, he did it willingly and without comment. He even seemed sympathetic, perhaps because he, too, was struggling against bodily impulses. That fall, for unknown reasons, Bilbo had begun lifting his leg on my mother's best furniture, soaking her decorative chair skirts and rusting the buttons on her blue velour sofa. Mom responded by demanding that "the dog" spend most of its time outdoors on a chain or locked in the garage. That's where I usually found him after school, barking frantically. I'd set him free and we'd go for a long walk, usually to the North Woods, where the physical world remained unchanged.

I should've guessed even that was temporary. One afternoon, Bilbo and I arrived at the woods to find half of it leveled, a grimy, still-warm bulldozer resting among the frayed and broken trunks. The creek had been stomped into muck and our shelter, our beloved refuge, had completely vanished. We charged home and confronted my mother with the disastrous news, to which she calmly replied, "They're just making room for more houses."

"More houses?" I snapped. "Who in their right mind would want to live in this dump of a town?"

"Now, John," she said. "We can't always make the world the way we'd like it to be."

"Yeah, unless you're an idiot with a bulldozer!"

I ran upstairs, lay down on the bed with Bilbo, and bawled.

It was a small miracle that when the state drama competition approached that winter, I was asked to play Felix Unger in a one-act duet from Neil Simon's *The Odd Couple*. Chaz had been cast as Oscar and I learned later that he'd requested me as his partner, which was the only reason Mr. Beck had agreed to it. Midway through our initial rehearsal—the famous spaghetti scene—Mr. Beck interjected that we were performing "like a couple of mating raccoons!" and stormed out of the room. This constructive criticism inspired Chaz and me to spend many additional hours rehearsing after school and at his house on the weekends. Chaz was serious about his acting career and, in fact, would be the most successful of all of Mr. Beck's students. He would later play roles on *The X-Files, Malcolm in the Middle, Ally McBeal,* and other television shows, as well as the lead in a *Hallmark Hall of Fame* greeting-card commercial. Real talent and ambition fueled his efforts. All I had, it seemed, was resentment and the desperate desire not to disappoint a friend who, against all reason, had rescued me from isolation and despair.

Other male members of Drama Club regularly joined us in Chaz's basement, attracted by the opportunity for additional rehearsal and by Chaz's mountain of audiovisual equipment. This included a top-of-the-line stereo system, computers, and a camera, which we used to record countless comedy skits and music videos. It was no different the night before sectionals, which we all spent at Chaz's house. After rehearsals, Chaz warmed up his shortwave radio transmitter—KFRT—and we spent much of the night broadcasting vulgar witticisms and German punk music to listeners within a five-block radius. The phone line was kept open for requests, but there were none.

At three or so in the morning, I cleared a sleeping space on the shag carpet among the pop cans and grease-stained pizza boxes. It was February, when Iowa basements tend to be cold, so I pulled a blanket over my shoulders. Unbeknownst to me, the blanket belonged to Chaz's dog, Trevor—a huge, fully-puffed chow—and it wasn't long before he was on top of me, gnawing my skull. I called for help, but the others were filming a music video for the Scorpions' "Blackout," which was cranked to top volume. I managed to push Trevor away and crawl to safety under the pullout sofa bed. The others eventually found places to sleep and Chaz turned out the lights.

"Hey, where's Price?" he asked.

And that's when it happened.

"Hee-hee-hee," I cackled, scratching at the bottom of the mattress. "Mole Man!"

"What the hell?" he said, and everyone burst into laughter.

I suppose they thought I was just being funny or trying to relieve the pressure of tomorrow's competition—that's what I thought, anyway. But there were other reasons Mole Man had reemerged from the space beneath the mattress, from the darkest recesses of my mind. I had little time to reflect on this, however. The next morning's competition began early, and despite the lack of sleep, we performed well. Even Mr. Beck was pleasantly surprised. Chaz and I received a "1" rating, which meant we'd be advancing to the state competition in March. So would the other duets—*I'm Herbert* and *Night Watch*—as well as our Readers' Theatre performance of *Death Cell*. Only one of our entries, a female mime duet entitled "The Zoo," didn't make it. We weren't sorry for them. Those girls had clearly found better things to do with their free time than practice acting like elephants and baboons.

After the competition it was back to reality, which for us drama boys meant standing in the corner of the main hallway, complaining. We were disappointed there'd been no official announcement of our nearly sweeping victory at sectionals. Instead, the school was busily preparing for Twirp Dance. This was our annual Valentine's dance, and the girls were required to ask the guys and pay for dinner. Hence, T.W.I.R.P.—The Woman Is Required to Pay. Almost all the girls in Drama Club had landed a date, and we were not among them. Only one of us guys had been asked and his date attended St. Edmund's, the Catholic High School, where our social status was largely unknown. I shouldn't have blamed those girls for my loneliness, but I did, bitterly. By that time the acne medication had kicked in and my face had temporarily erupted into large scabs that tended to flake off during conversations. No one wanted to eat lunch with me, let alone slow-dance.

Even without the scabs, I'm not sure things would've been any different. The girls I knew were used to overlooking me by then, a tiny blip that had long ago vanished from their collective radar. The last and only time I'd been asked to a dance was in eighth grade, a student council party held at the popular Rainforest disco. My date, Liz, was cute and barely taller than me, but deaf. In order to dance, she needed to feel the vibrations of the music, which required standing very close to the massive floor speakers—an excruciating experience that did untold damage to my own hearing. Plus, I was so short that whenever they released the dry ice (which was often, as this was a rainforest) I became blinded and choked by the low-lying fog. In the midst of one of those deafening clouds, I knocked Liz's glasses off her face and spent the rest of the song searching for them on my hands and knees. She opted to pursue other romantic interests and, again, who could blame her?

The highlight of our Valentine festivities, besides the dance, was the crowning of the Twirp King during a Friday assembly. A week or so beforehand, the drama gang was standing in the hallway, complaining about how ridiculous the whole thing was, this popularity contest masquerading as an "election." "Whatever happened to the school's scholastic mission?" one of us asked, earnestly. "Whatever happened to *priorities?*" The pitch of our discussion was particularly high due in part to the final, collective realization that only one of us would be attending the dance. But it was also due to the recent public abuse of Doug, our youngest and (now) shortest member. During band practice, while the teacher was temporarily called to the office, a pack of seniors had chased and "depantsed" Doug, forcing him to run half naked in front of the heckling crowd. I had witnessed this humiliation, helpless and in horror, while hiding behind my French horn. Doug had been absent from class for most of that week and we worried he might never return. When the band turns on you, you've hit bottom.

"Well, why don't we do something about it?" Chaz said. "Why don't we nominate our own Twirp King candidate?"

"Like who?" I snorted, looking around at that meager collection of tortoiseshell glasses, tight corduroys, and Hush Puppies.

"How about you, Mole Man?"

I snorted again, but the general response was overwhelmingly enthusiastic. Above my head, they began exchanging ideas and strategies, and by the end of lunch a rough plan was drafted. Drama Club was graced with several boys skilled in the use of mixed media, including prominent members of the school newspaper and yearbook. They volunteered to print off posters and flyers, while others agreed to work on distribution—there wasn't much time, so it would have to be quick and, of course, dramatic. I was reluctant to go along at first, even though they swore I'd be anonymous and that the campaign would make a positive difference in the lives of our fellow students. Besides, Chaz added, it would be hilarious—a grand joke on the dumbasses running this carnival of horrors. It was this latter argument that finally swayed me, betraying what was truly at stake for all of us: *Revenge!*

Later that week, after rehearsal, we scurried like vermin through the empty hallways. We draped the cafeteria walls with huge posters printed on green-and-white-striped, perforated computer paper. Each giant letter of every giant word was composed of hundreds of tiny letters that our digital expert had tried, unsuccessfully, to make spell out *UP* and *YOURS.* Smaller posters were taped to the doors of the classrooms, the restrooms, and even the principal's office. Colorful "mole prints" were stuck to the lockers of the other Twirp candidates and anyone else we had reason to hate or resent, which was most of the student body. The effort left us exhausted—revenge is thirsty work—so afterward we piled into my olive green Buick Electra and headed to a local hamburger joint. Sitting on the cold Naugahyde of an isolated booth, we toasted the beginning of our crusade. The beginning of a new world.

Next morning, students were confronted everywhere by our rallying cries: "Vote for Mole Man!" "Mole Man IS a Twirp!" "King Mole!" "Mole Man Can Pay, Baby!" We heard their talk, their wonderment—"Who is this mysterious Mole Man?"— and were encouraged beyond expression. One of us had begun

circulating the "mole call"—a high-pitched "hee-hee-hee"—and
it was gaining steam in the hallways, locker rooms, and cafeteria. As were our campaign songs: "Who can it be now? *Mole
Man!*" and "*Alles klar, Herr* Mole*hssar?*" and "It's a nice day for
a *mole* wedding! It's a nice day to start again!" The campaign was
picked up by other geeks and foreign exchangers who seemed to
have found courage in our efforts. Some tried to distribute campaign flyers in the hallway, only to have them crumpled and
tossed back into their faces. Our posters were similarly vandal-
ized and one thug dumped a bunch of our "mole prints" into
the boys' urinals. We refused to be discouraged. During the
darkest hours, I recalled the defiant words of my comic book inspiration: "Witless youth! Laugh while you may! Soon, your humor will change to FEAR!"

Indeed, on election morn, the geek who read announce-
ments over the PA system reminded us to vote for Twirp King.
"And remember," he concluded, "you can always vote for a
write-in candidate. Like, maybe . . . *Mole Man! Hee-hee-hee!*"
The speaker instantly went dead, but the success of our infiltra-
tion was clear. I cast my ballot with murderous glee.

<hr>

All this makes me want to believe something supernatural was
behind my encounter with a real-life mole, that very winter. I'd
also like to believe that it occurred the same week as the Twirp
King campaign, but that may also be fantasy. What I remember
for sure is that it was an unusually warm winter day, and Bilbo
and I were outside tossing the stick. At one point I noticed
something squirming on the ground near the retaining wall.

Bilbo charged over and I barely restrained him from biting it in half. The sight froze my blood. This mole—perhaps awakened by the warm weather or by Bilbo's digging in the adjacent garden or by some unknown affliction—had worked its way through a gap in the retaining wall and fallen onto the driveway, where it was now scraping the soggy gravel with its pink webby bat claws. I thought I'd seen a mole before, thought I knew all about them—they were small and cute and courageous, like Moley in *The Wind in the Willows*—but this thing was huge and grotesque, with matted gray fur and spots of raw, exposed flesh. One of its eyes appeared to have been plucked from the socket. Part rat, part frog, part mange-diseased kitten, it reminded me of the mercury-deformed monster in the horror movie *Prophecy*, or one of Mole Man's subterranean gargoyles, or something that had crawled out of that Hieronymus Bosch painting of Hell. This was no Moley, no congenial spirit animal. This was a creature of unspeakably dark powers, an embodiment of the netherworld, of the living dead—of pestilence and perversion and rage.

My first impulse, like Bilbo's, was to kill it. But then another idea infected me. I chained the still barking dog to the tree, scooped the mole into a bucket, and headed to the North Woods. The decimation there was starker in the winter, and it had progressed, encroaching on the hill where our benevolent god, the woodchuck, had once ruled. Squirming in my bucket, however, was another kind of god, jealous and vengeful; one who, unlike another I sometimes believed in, might go a long way toward restoring and protecting the wild spirit of that place, as well as my own. For months I'd fantasized about ways to vandalize the construction site, usually involving corn syrup and explosives, but here was the more effective weapon—alive and intelligent and pissed. I took a moment to imagine the mole and its fetid offspring wreaking havoc in the future yards of those abominations referred to, without irony, as modern homes. Expensive lawn repairs, crumbling driveways, broken ankles—the possibilities were endless. When I released the mole on the upturned earth, it began digging and slowly disappeared. I watched the soil pulse in its wake, until it became a small, nearly indistinguishable shiver.

That night in bed, feeling satisfied, I apologized to Bilbo for chaining him to the tree. I assured him it was for a good cause, but he was not in a trusting mood, panting and gazing pensively at the door. He was worried about my mother, I suppose, and he had good reason. Although Bilbo appeared to have stopped peeing on the furniture, he had recently acquired the more odious habit of humping everything in sight: bed comforters, the grandfather clock, small children—even me, if I wasn't careful. In an attempt to redirect his interests, my mother had purchased a leopard-spotted throw pillow at a garage sale. The moment Bilbo started in on a visitor's leg, Mom would command one of us to drag him to the back porch, where he could finish the job on the pillow. Within a month, he was volunteering most of his time out there.

Then it became my parents' turn to host bridge club. Mom and Dad weren't big socializers, so bridge club offered a rare opportunity to invite their closest friends into our home, show off the crystal, pour some wine, and enjoy an evening of grown-up elegance. The success of this event depended to no small extent on our absence from it. My sisters and I were instructed to remain upstairs, dressed in Sunday clothes, until Mom invited us to greet everyone. On this particular evening, however, when we were called downstairs, Bilbo charged down with us. He shot past my mother, rushed to the porch, dragged the leopard pillow into the middle of the family room floor, and there, in front of the bank president's wife, made furious love to it. I started to laugh, but the look on my mother's face stopped me cold. She calmly requested that I take Bilbo upstairs, which I did, immediately.

During the days that followed, it became clear that my mother had completely detached from Bilbo. It didn't matter how wronged I thought he'd been or that he'd "given it his best" or that he'd simply been following instinct. From that moment on, whatever else Bilbo did or didn't do, my mother could no longer love that dog; she could only tolerate him. And I knew even then that to be merely tolerated often meant you were the first to die—Mom had, in fact, casually suggested our dog might be happier on "a farm." Bilbo seemed to sense the danger, huddling against my rib cage at night, peering at the bedroom door. Lying with him on the covers during Twirp week, I listened to my mother's footsteps in the kitchen, wondering again that such a change was possible in her. If a dog's poor behavior could provoke this transformation in my mother—a woman who loved nature, who'd rescued countless animals from death—then couldn't it happen in anyone, toward anyone? Even me?

On the way to Friday's Twirp assembly, I was full of new doubts. Not about the election—victory was a real possibility—but rather, about the vengeful impulses that had inspired me to participate in the first place. Was this how I wanted to be remembered by my peers, however stupid they might be? Was this the legacy I wanted to hand down to the next generation of marginalized youth? If so, what would be the consequences—for me, for them, for the world? My buddies appeared to have no such misgivings. They were talking excitedly among themselves: Do you think we won? Do you think we taught them a lesson? What shall we do next—deflate tires, put Nair in the football helmets, sprinkle cesium into the swimming pool and watch it explode? I scanned the packed auditorium—What would I say to them during my victory speech? What message would I deliver, knowing that it might someday come back around to find me?

The student body president approached the mike. "Welcome to our Twirp King celebration!" she declared. "We would like to dedicate today's assembly to the mysterious Mole Man, whoever he may be."

There were scattered cheers and applause, quickly overwhelmed by boos. *Oh my god,* I thought. *I've actually won.* I started to stand, but Chaz grabbed my arm—the ceremony was only beginning. The theme was "Fantasy Island," and the various candidates, at least those without a secret identity, were required to dress up as rock stars arriving on the D-plane, as they did on the television show. There was Alice Cooper, Elvis, Kiss drummer Peter Chris, Meatloaf, Devo, Ted Nugent, Stray Cats singer Brian Setzer, and a cross-dressing Dolly Parton. All were welcomed by Mr. Roark and Tattoo—played by a girl waddling around on her knees—and a gaggle of hula dancers. Each candidate was required to perform a short clip from one of his or her hit songs—"School's Out for Summer," "Whip It," "9 to 5," and so on—after which the crowd went wild. I rolled my eyes at the applause these dorks were enjoying but had to admit, as actors, they weren't half bad. At the end of it all, when Elvis left the stage, I expected the victorious Mole Man finally to be called from the audience. The panic roiled within me: What would I say to them? Our student body president stepped to the front of the stage, raised the Twirp King's golden crown into the air, moved slowly up and down the line of candidates, and finally dropped it on the head of Alice Cooper. The crowd erupted with cheers and applause, followed by an encore performance from Alice, and then it was over.

Twirp Dance was held the next night as scheduled. Mole Man campaign posters were torn down and replaced with streamers and sparkle balls—or so we'd been told. Of the dance itself, I could only wonder, but here's how it was later described in the yearbook:

> After the outrageous Twirp assembly, the guys looked forward to a free night out with the girls. Most of the girls cashed their checks and ran out to the Crossroads Mall for a new outfit Friday after school. What little money was left from their shopping spree was thrown in their purses, and then their excitement grew as they set out the latest additions to their wardrobes. Saturday night, the last adjustments to face and hair were made and after a frantic search for the car keys, the girls were ready to go. . . . The dates were picked up, parents were met and pictures were taken. The girls were finally getting a taste of what guys have been going through

for years. Everybody at the dance was in high spirits and ready to party. The girls were decked out in the latest spring fashions including mini-skirts, polka-dots, pin-stripes, and bow ties. Pyramid was the night's entertainment and they cranked out the tunes as everybody danced the night away to Van Halen, Ozzy Ozborne, and Billy Squire. As the dance came to a close, the girls emptied their purses in order to scrounge up enough money for food. Everyone scattered to various restaurants and hit the parties at Holiday Inn and Towers later on. Early morning curfews were stretched and a good time was had by all.

"Give it up," Chaz told me at his house that weekend. "Things'll change." He was right, in a way. In less than a month, the pimples and scabs would clear and I'd meet my first serious girlfriend. We'd be together for over a year, during which I'd gain another couple of inches and a lot of confidence. Chaz would graduate and I'd quit Drama Club in favor of the tennis team, hanging out with new, more popular friends. I'd put away the comic books and take up painting exotic, faraway landscapes with Aunt Esther—the places where I dreamed of living someday. All this left little time to spend alone in my room or with Bilbo. The next summer, just before leaving for college, I would return from Ragbrai, an annual bicycle ride across Iowa, to discover that Mom had given Bilbo to a "farmer friend." I could still visit him, she said, but I never did.

The Mole Man campaign, like my shorter self, like my dog, would soon become memory. But the animals that inhabit our adolescent spirits never entirely abandon us. In the decades to follow, I'd often recall the affection and generosity of Bilbo, and hope for his forgiveness. As for Mole Man, his injuries and ambitions had indelibly become my own, and deep down, in the cold subterranean sources of my ethical life, he'd continue to wield influence. *It all started long ago,* I'd tell myself and others many times, in many ways, for many different reasons. *Because the people of the surface world mocked me!*

No, I'd never give it up. And certainly not during Twirp weekend, at Chaz's house, where several other members of Drama Club eventually dropped by. When Chaz warmed up the KFRT transmitter, I felt the vindictive zeal once again heat within me. There we were, Mole Man and his minions, underground, preparing to use technology to subvert the stock cruelty and self-indulgent materialism of the surface world, calling others to our cause. They were out there, I could sense it, hiding like us in their basements and bedrooms, their talents unappreciated, their pain unacknowledged, their powers unrealized. When the microphone buzzed, I let out a defiant Mole Call— *hee, hee, hee*—which earned a raucous cheer from my friends. But the call was not intended for them; it was for the ones out there, in our town and beyond, across the black abyss of space and time, where it would become—Who could know?—the voice of hope or ruin.

In the meantime, the lines were open. We waited for the requests to pour in, but there were none. Only our own, and we played them, repeatedly and without shame, all night long.

NYMPH

The leaves of the oak had turned caramel brown, dropping onto my book, my journal, onto the warped, paint-scabbed surface of the picnic table in College Green Park, Iowa City. I occasionally brushed them away, a far less annoying chore than brushing away mosquitoes and gnats—like most of the insects, they were gone now. The incessant summer drone of cicadas had been silenced. Only the birds and squirrels were left to make noise from the branches of the tree, a massive spread that broke the October sun into a million gold pieces, tossing them across the table, my arms, the grass. Beneath the table, I rested my foot on a thick tubular root, while a soft northeastern wind riffled the pages of my book.

I was supposed to be reading a short story, and like most of the stories assigned in that introductory lit course, it was about death: "The Death of Iván Ilých." But I was having trouble focusing: It was a beautiful fall day, there were children playing in the park, leaves were rustling in the breeze, and I was a sophomore. So I put death aside and focused, as our professor had encouraged us to, on something "immediate and/or personally relevant." Iván, the dying protagonist, was being mistreated by his doctors, which was personally relevant because I had decided to become a doctor. Why I had decided this was a question I'd been increasingly asking myself. One version involved a girl, a very tall girl whom I'd met during freshman orientation. While we were holding hands in the dormitory stairwell, she'd told me she was going to play center for the Hawkeyes, and I took a moment to picture ten thousand people cheering as my girl-friend—the tallest, most popular girl on campus—swatted a basketball into someone's face. She told me she was going to be a doctor, and the next thing I knew I'd signed on for four years of advanced chemistry, biology, and mathematics.

My mother and my grandmother Kathryn were, of course, thrilled with the possibility of a doctor in the family. For me, though, serious doubts emerged just a few weeks into the semes-ter, when the basketball player stuffed our courtship—perhaps afraid of injuring her back while stooping for a kiss. Shortly af-ter, I registered for a spring religion course specifically designed to confuse students engaged, as I now seemed to be, in curricu-lums devoid of personal fulfillment. The title of the course was "Quest for Human Destiny," and the professor was a passion-ate, muscular rabbi who boasted a black belt in Tai Kwon Do and a fierce, unapologetic love for the Philadelphia 76ers. He began the semester with the modest proposal that God, in the Genesis story, intended Adam and Eve to eat the forbidden fruit from the Tree of Knowledge of Good and Evil. Why else place it in the very center of the Garden of Eden? Why else create the snake that he knew would tempt Eve? The exit from Eden, rather than a fall into sin, was a divinely ordained ascension from dumb existence into the difficult, but necessary, world of ethical choices.

After debunking what I'd thought was the foundation of Judeo-Christian belief, our professor casually moved on to *The Epic of Gilgamesh, Siddhartha, The Old Man and the Sea, The Catcher in the Rye,* and two films, *2001: A Space Odyssey* and *A Clockwork Orange.* The pace and style of his lectures were as athletic as he was, his voice often rising to a shout, his neck veins and biceps bulging—the man clearly cared about the ideas he taught. From my seat at the top of the balcony, in that over-crowded, musty auditorium, I watched and listened, taking voracious notes, completely enthralled. Until then, intellectual and artistic ambition had too often been an occasion for mockery and failure. During my senior year of high school, for instance, my father had decided to treat the whole family to *The Epic of Gilgamesh,* as performed by the touring National Theatre of the Deaf. During this completely silent performance, someone in the auditorium belched loudly and repeatedly, enraging my father but sending others into silent spasms of laughter that lasted pretty much the entire show.

In "Quest for Human Destiny," I was reading and rereading that same ancient story, lost in the adventures of the King of Uruk as he felled the giant sacred cedar, slew the monster guardian of the forest, then the Bull of Heaven, then the lions in the passes of the mountains. Finally, after losing his hairy best friend and surrogate brother Enkidu to a long illness, Gilgamesh attempted to defeat death itself. He traveled to the island of the immortal Utnapishtim, the Sumerian Noah, who told a tale of worldwide deluge nearly identical to the one in

Genesis, though our professor said it may have preceded the Biblical version by centuries. Unlike the story of Noah, which ends with the happy return of the dove carrying an olive leaf and then God's rainbow, the version in *Gilgamesh* ends with the release of the raven, which, because of massive amounts of carrion, does not choose to return—the more realistic picture of worldwide destruction, I thought. Death and despair are the end result of the flood, as well as the end of Gilgamesh's quest to achieve immortality. The hero proclaims, "[M]isery comes at last to the healthy man, the end of life is sorrow."

That pretty much summed up my attitude during those initial, lonely midwinter weeks of the semester—and much of my adolescence to date. The readings and lectures in that course, however, fanned a spark of intellectual joy that helped sustain me the rest of my first year in college. Before I departed for the summer, my premed adviser encouraged me to declare a major in the humanities; medical schools were partial to "academically diverse applicants," she said—so I chose Religion.

When I returned to Iowa City after a summer spent working the night shift at the Fort Dodge Hardees (speaking of death and despair), the increased amount of reading in my humanities courses forced me to seek out new, more humane places for study. Although I'd moved from the dorms into an apartment with three studious friends, the view from my bedroom desk was of a brick wall. Ralston Creek, for which our apartments were named, flowed invisibly behind a nearby auto body shop, but its primary function was to attract mosquitoes and rats, one of whom I regularly confronted outside our apartment door, munching cigarettes and piercing me with a Clint Eastwood glare: *Are you feeling lucky, punk?* As for the library, I'd had no trouble studying math equations and molecular structures in the isolation chamber known as fifth floor, but I'd discovered during "Quest for Human Destiny" that it was impossible for me to read literature there. Perhaps this was due to the sensory deprivation or the fact that, halfway into the first paragraph of anything artful, I'd inevitably fall asleep and wake facedown in a nest of drool-soaked, engorged pages. I tried popping caffeine pills but gave them up when, during one late-night study session, I repeatedly hallucinated the trumpet score from *The Waltons*.

Further trials suggested that the open air was more conducive to reading, but I had trouble locating the ideal habitat. Sitting along the Iowa River, I was too often distracted by the disturbing mating rituals of ducks and other coeds. Local restaurants had an annoying habit of letting only paying customers occupy their sidewalk tables, and as far as I knew, outdoor espresso stands had yet to roll across state borders. One night I climbed the fire escape to the top of Seashore Hall, where I used a flashlight to read beneath the stars. I was eventually escorted back down by campus police, concerned that my perusing of *Hamlet* while perched eight stories high might be a sign of suicidal impulses.

I began taking long walks beyond campus, searching, laying claim to the odd sidewalk bench or footbridge or backyard gazebo, getting chased by barking dogs, until I discovered College Green Park. It was a small neighborhood green space located on a hill, with a great view and lots of trees, and occupied mostly by quiet couples and children climbing on the play set or being pushed on the swings by their parents. I settled at one of the ancient picnic tables, beneath that enormous oak tree, and in some ways never left.

Before sitting down that day to read "The Death of Iván Ilých," I explored, as usual, the circumference of the tree, so wide I doubt three men could link arms around it. I'd tried to climb it a few times, but made it only halfway up the trunk before losing my grip, and some of the flesh off my knees, as I slid to the ground. Its branches remained the exclusive domain of crows and squirrels, whose noisy scolding was an occasional source of distraction. As was the possibility of finding the dried husks of cicada nymphs clinging to its gnarly bark—I regularly searched for them, a habit carried over from childhood. These were the dried skins, abandoned by the cicadas when they morphed and grew wings, though the husks perfectly retained their old forms. On that day I found three of them midway up the trunk, as if their own frustrated efforts to climb had been the final inspiration to leave their earthly bodies and take flight.

I set the cicada nymphs alongside the pages of Tolstoy, where they appeared to be keeping bedside vigil, forelegs crossed in prayer. Inside those pages, Iván, a professionally successful family man with a mysterious affliction, soon came to the frightening end of self-deception: "[S]omething terrible, new, and more important than anything before in his life, was taking place within him of which he alone was aware." *His doctors should have been aware,* I wrote in my reading journal, where I continued to focus on the medical mishaps, harshly condemning their misdiagnoses—one blamed a floating spleen, the other a sick appendix—and their insensitive, useless treatments. *How ironic,* I wrote, because irony was something of which our professor approved, *that the servant, Gerasim, is more effective at relieving Iván's suffering, just by letting him rest his legs on his shoulders.*

But Iván's death was inevitable—the title sort of gave it away—and it wasn't long before that theme returned to the center of my concern. Death was, in a way, the more "immediate and/or personally relevant" topic. Yes, it was a lovely fall day, I was young, but there were those hollowed-out cicada eyes staring at me, the distinct chill in the air, the leaves dropping onto my book. A dead branch had fallen just to the left of the table, where a myriad of insects was likely hatching out of the damp undersides. Grandpa Roy had corralled me into picking up a number of similar branches in our yard back home, exposing similar myriads, after a storm or one of his enthusiastic prunings. He and I had planted several of those trees together, including the silver maple and blue spruce in the front, and the apple in back. His death from a heart attack during my junior year in high school was sudden and, like others I'd known, beyond sight. One Saturday in November he took us all out to Country Kitchen for breakfast, plugging the jukebox to play "Lucille" by Kenny Rogers because the waitress was named Lucille. He insisted, as usual, on refilling the coffee cups of customers in neighboring booths, his palsied hand splashing hot liquid onto their table and sometimes their laps. The next Saturday I was looking down at him in the casket and slipping a dollar bill into his shirt pocket, as he'd done for me so many times: "In case you get thirsty for a pop." The emotional and physical facts of death were real enough—mortuary art only amplified them—but the act of dying, the transition from there to here, as well as the possibility of delaying or even stopping that transition, remained a troubling mystery.

My science textbooks, piled on the same picnic table as Tolstoy, were doing their best to rob me of this ignorance: Memorizing molecular structures was its own kind of death. Yet, for all the anxiety associated with premed courses, they'd begun to instill in me a profound appreciation of the beauty, complexity, and fragility of the human body. These stood in stark contrast to my own self-conception, and to those of many around me. University life, especially inside the dormitories, had appeared at times to be one giant, collective experiment in physical debasement, both real and symbolic. One of my dormitory roommates had had the habit, when drunk and asleep, of showering urine onto the other roommate sleeping in the bunk below. Meanwhile, our intramural basketball team had dubbed itself "Sticky Fingers," and the captain of our flag football team had nicknamed me "Hymen" because, as a defensive back, I'd so often failed to prevent penetration.

The electron-microscopic photos inside my biology textbooks revealed the body to be an immense landscape of variety and grandeur. Individual red blood cells, corpulent and smooth, or flowering, squid-armed neurons were so beautiful that their casual loss from a stubbed toe or too much Milwaukee's Best seemed the heights of tragedy. Bacteria, mold spores, and germs—perhaps the same ones thriving in the dormitory urinals—also achieved a certain dignity when viewed up close. Even death and decay, the very sources of human misery, were at the cellular level an exquisite dance of violence, transformation, and rebirth.

Whatever motivations I'd had for becoming a doctor, they weren't entirely superficial. My mother was a special-education nurse, and I'd sometimes traveled with her to rural schools, at the end of long roads through the corn, to check on children with feeding tubes or lice or sores from sitting in wheelchairs all day. I'd seen what it meant to alleviate physical suffering. Nothing I'd since encountered in my science and humanities courses suggested that a lifetime of studying the beauty of the body, ministering to its needs, wasn't an admirable vision of my future.

So why didn't I feel I belonged there?

This was a question I'd asked myself before, but it returned to me with renewed force that afternoon as I read about poor Iván on his deathbed. That's where the story seemed to put me as well, on my own deathbed, shaded by the tree, attended by reverent cicada nymphs. This shouldn't have been the big deal it was. Death had been a theme in plenty of other humanities courses, including "Quest for Human Destiny," where even the giant fetus at the end of *2001: A Space Odyssey* was, according to our professor, an alien instrument of apocalypse. This story, however, put me inside a specific death, one that lasted several excruciating months and over a hundred pages. It made me a little sick, to tell the truth: the sour reflux in his mouth, the increasing pain in his side, the growing regret over the "scarcely noticeable impulses" ignored during a lifetime. The kind of regret that made him question whether his "professional duties and the whole arrangement of his life and of his family, and of all his social and official interests might all have been false."

Iván's story seemed headed toward another "all is sorrow" ending, and at some point before the final pages, I felt compelled to walk away from it. I passed the other trees dropping colorful leaves on picnic tables, the children swinging and playing, until I came to the western border. From that high spot, I looked down on the leafy canopy of Iowa City, punctured by church steeples and downtown buildings and, in the far distance, the golden dome of the old state capital. Just beneath it, I knew, were a bunch of gingko trees, a species as old as the dinosaurs, also turning gold and dropping their rancid seed pods on the sidewalks of the Pentacrest. Freshmen could always be spotted on those sidewalks, frantically checking the bottom of their shoes for what smelled suspiciously like dog crap.

I'd done the same thing myself the year before. How terrified I'd been during those first weeks at the university, which surprised me at the time. My parents had both graduated from the University of Iowa, and I'd visited the campus to attend Hawkeye football games and high school events. Iowa City was almost as familiar as Fort Dodge, which was another reason I'd wanted to attend university out of state. I'd applied to a modest group of them—Harvard, Duke, Berkeley—but apparently my high school grades weren't good enough to draw much attention, let alone financial aid. Now, barely a year into my stay, it had become a place of increasingly particular character, to blend with my own. The rain-darkened, classical facade of the Chem-Botany building; the first snow on the Iowa River, viewed from a steamy window in the student union; my picnic table in the park—these and other places were quickly becoming sites of memory, and not always pleasant ones. Inside my college books and courses, I was being exposed to the broader canvas of the planet's history—its evolutions and extinctions, its ongoing human and environmental suffering. The meaning of the question—*What should I do?*—was growing into something more than vocational. Fort Dodge, for all its troubles, had been a kind of shelter from which I'd emerged into a strange existence full of difficult and urgent choices. What exactly those choices were, however, still seemed beyond my reach.

I returned to my spot beneath the tree, resolved at least to see poor Iván through to his miserable end. There was more suffering, more regret, and then rage at the "falsity" of those around him getting on with their lives—his daughter becoming engaged, his wife attending opera, his friends playing bridge—while he suffered. The rage (and hadn't I already felt this, despite my sheltered life?) at the "cruelty of man, the cruelty of God, the absence of God." Finally, while screaming in pain, Iván's flailing hand falls on the head of his young son, who takes it and kisses it, crying. Through that accidental gesture, Iván becomes aware of the torment his dying has caused his family and decides to release them: "Take him away . . ." he says to his wife, "sorry for him . . . sorry for you too." When he tries to say, "Forgive me," the words get jumbled, but the effort itself becomes the light that redeems his life, defeats his suffering and death—"What joy!" In the end, the one who believed himself so mistreated—by his doctors, his body, his community, his God—heals himself and others through a couple of words, given in love.

Later, I would look back on this moment as perhaps the beginning of my journey as a writer. At the time, though, I had no idea what shape my life would assume or how far that life would carry me or what difference I could possibly make. I only knew that something significant had shifted inside me. I pushed Iván's story aside, along with my other books, and stretched out on top of the picnic table. I gazed into the branches of the oak. Seen one way, the branches appeared to be arms holding up the sky. Seen another, they became roots extending into an icy void. Some of the branches stretched out parallel to the earth, while others shot straight up or down. Others appeared to twist, even curl, having reversed and corrected themselves over the course of decades, maybe a century lived in that one spot—long enough for the scars and broken places to give birth to interesting formations, faces and landscapes, and pools of water to which squirrels and birds and insects came to drink.

I shifted my weight and heard a small crunch. I reached my hand over, found the forgotten cicadas, and lifted them one by one onto my chest. At close range, their individual features, like those of the branches, became clear: the distinct lobes and ridges of the thorax, the stunned look of the eyes, the final gesture of their crablike pincers. I didn't know enough to tell whether they were the famous seventeen-year cicadas or your basic dog-day variety. Either way, they'd spent years underground, feeding on the roots of the tree, my tree, growing into nymphs, emerging, climbing, transforming into winged selves that had scratched out their songs and long since died. This was all that was left of them now, these husks, brown and fragile and translucent, like parchment.

When I got up to leave, the nymphs continued to cling to the fabric of my shirt, even the damaged one, just a head and forearms. They held on, along with a leaf or two, as I packed up my books and left the park. By the time I reached my apartment they were gone. Only a mile or so, but farther than any of us could've expected.

Titan

I watched as first light slowly carved out the saddle of the Santa Rita Mountains. My family and I had flown into Tucson during the night, during the first Christmas blizzard there in thirty-some years. While Grandma Kathryn drove us south from the airport to their home in Green Valley, I could see nothing of the land itself. Snow—great gobs of it—was falling into the light of the highway lamps, just as it had been when we left Des Moines. Now, in the growing dawn, the snow was resting like fur stoles on the shoulders of the saguaros, though it was already starting to melt. All of winter in a night. The desert was beginning to reassert itself: its dry ascending angles, its spiny, ground-scratching fertility. I still couldn't believe I was there, in the Sonora.

Across the room, hanging above the bed, I spotted a painting of Grandpa Andy and me. We are sitting together on a stone bench, watching swans glide across the Northlawn Cemetery pond in Fort Dodge, where he'd lived all of his life until moving to Arizona when I was nine. I am probably six years old in that painting and my grandfather in his sixties, but the artist—

Grandpa's sister, Esther—has captured the similar slope of our shoulders and even the smaller trait of attached earlobes. There is an oak tree, a branch extending above our heads, its leaves drooping from the humidity. The scene reminded me of home, a child's summer.

But it was the snow outside, not the summer inside, that exerted the strongest pull toward my grandfather. It is often winter in my earliest memories of him, after a big blizzard, like the one in 1975, when he was required to be at the Gas and Electric service garage all day and into the night to monitor the trucks. I begged to spend time with him, and the trucks, so he'd pick me up just after supper when the horizon held a ribbon of gold beneath the blackness. I'd gaze out the pickup window at the last strings of Christmas lights, red and green, dangling from this house or that, and listen to the cold crunch of the snow beneath the tires. I felt warm and safe. When we entered the garage I'd see the hulked shadows of men, striding around or bent over engines, in the dry heat, in the honeyed, whiskey-colored light. *Good workers,* my grandfather always called them, and the tone of his voice made me believe there was something magical about it, like if you worked that hard, you could erase all your mistakes and sins.

Grandpa and I would walk the line of trucks, and when we came to the biggest, the one with the crane folded over it like a giant spider's leg, he'd grab me under the armpits and lift me into the dark cabby. "Time to go to work, Tiger," he'd say, "and don't look at any of those magazines under the seat." When he disappeared into the office, I'd put on the yellow hard hat, cross my hands on the center of the wheel, and pause to savor the oily leather smell of the interior. Then, with all my strength, I'd press down, unleashing a blast of trumpets to startle the men, to shake the foundations of the garage, the earth.

"Did you notice Esther's painting?" Grandma asked as she poured me a glass of orange juice. "I hung it there for you. You are so special to your grandfather. Do you remember how he used to call you 'Tiger' and took you to the garage to honk the horns and how you begged him to read 'The House That Jack Built'—*This is the cat that ate the mouse that ate the grain that . . .*" Her list was overly familiar and I tuned it out. I was anxious to read the sports page before the rest of my family awakened. Across from me, Grandpa's chair was empty, but his cereal bowl had already been filled with raisin bran. A gritty cloud of Metamucil spun inside his glass. Grandpa had been asleep when we arrived the previous night, but now I could hear the buzz of his electric razor. "All he ever sees nowadays are old women," Grandma said, placing the silverware. "Since the stroke, the men in the neighborhood visit him less frequently. They don't like the way he looks," she said. "They don't know what to say."

"Thank goodness you're here for him."

I wanted to tell her that, actually, I'm here to relax after a difficult college semester, to go swimming and get a tan and impress my girlfriend with a postcard from someplace more exotic than the Iowa State Fair. But that wasn't exactly true, either. I was there because I wanted to see my grandparents, whom I loved and missed, though I couldn't help resisting Grandma's expectations. She believed that I was destined to save Grandpa, either through my future career as a doctor or just through the divine magic of my presence. I knew this because she'd told me so, many times, in letters and phone calls. *You're the boy he always wanted,* she'd say, often repeating the story of the infant son she'd miscarried on Grandpa's birthday, in that terrible snowstorm. *You're our miracle. Our gift from God.*

She handed me the newspaper: "You've always been a voracious reader, John. There's an editorial on the importance of prayer that will interest you. I've circled it in red."

She watched until I found the right page, then returned to the kitchen. I didn't read the editorial; she must've sent a hundred just like it in my college care packages, tucked between crumbled sugar cookies and tins of smoked almonds. I checked the basketball rankings instead—the Hawkeyes were still in the top twenty—then tried to determine the sort of social scene available to college-age kids like myself. I searched the paper two or three times and found no evidence of such a scene. No evidence of any young people at all. This surprised me. Every year my grandmother asked when we were going to travel to Arizona, citing neighbors, most of them from the Midwest, whose children and grandchildren visited more frequently. She told us this as if it was an embarrassment to be conspicuously alone in that place, without generational weight. That was the heart of the guilt she gave my mother—we didn't care enough. And yet the news of that community was delivered without that weight, as gray and thin as the paper it was printed on.

"Well, hello there, Tiger!"

Grandpa appeared in the doorway, clean-shaven and dressed in a pressed navy blue sweat suit—certainly not the repulsive figure described by the men who'd stopped visiting.

"What took you so long?" I asked. "Were you looking at those magazines under the truck seat, again?"

He laughed and then I noticed the changes: the way the left side of his face struggled with the smile, the slightly dimmer eyes, set deeper in the skull. He was leaning heavily on a walker, no longer the cane, unsure of the next step. I put down the paper, embraced him, and helped him to his chair.

An hour or so later, I was walking alone to the neighborhood pool in my new swim trunks and sandals. There was a slight chill in the air, but the snow was gone. Grandpa hadn't made it very far into our conversation after breakfast. We'd shared a few memories from my childhood, but he'd nodded off when I started talking about my college courses. I'd decided to let him sleep. The manicured lots they called yards were filled with white, decorative rocks and cacti pin cushion, rainbow, organ pipe—neatly arranged. There were several Saint Francis birdbaths and, in one yard, a herd of porcelain deer. A real quail scurried across the empty, quiet street while a rabbit stretched out in the shade of a palo verde tree. Grandma claimed a lot of people there didn't like palo verdes because, unlike cacti, they dropped leaves and created messes. I thought their yellow leaves were delicate and pretty, like flower petals scattered at a wedding.

This was not the desert I'd imagined as a child. A month or so after moving to Arizona, just before my grandfather's stroke, he'd sent me a colorful postcard entitled "Wildlife of the Desert." Drawn against the rocky backdrop of the Sonora had been a giant saguaro with an elf owl peeking out of a small, circular cavity, as well as a howling coyote, a horned toad, a Gila monster, and a sharp-fanged mountain lion crouching on a cliff, ready to pounce. There'd been a rattlesnake coiled in front of a human skull, just as Cousin Dave and I might've drawn it. Grandpa had scratched a black *x* by the snake because he'd seen a dead one on a golf course down there. He wrote that it was as big around as his arm, and that he would've cut off its rattle and sent it to me if someone hadn't told him it was poisonous. Even dead and cut to pieces that snake could've struck out and bit me—that's how powerful it was. You couldn't step anywhere in that picture without getting bit by something huge and deadly, it seemed. The black widow spider in the top corner had been drawn as big as the mule deer, the tarantula as big as the javelina, the scorpion as big as the quail. Back in Iowa, under a tent of covers, I'd obsessively studied that postcard, wondering that so many dangerous creatures could be crammed into one place. Why would anyone want to live there? Who wanted to bump into a rattlesnake on a golf course? Other times, after I'd turned out the lights, I'd lie back and feel the emptiness of the place where I lived, how there wasn't much danger left in it. And if there wasn't much danger in a place, what was there to make people pay attention and wonder about it? I dreamed of coyotes howling.

A golf cart honked as it passed and one of the men inside glared at me until it rounded the next corner. These were the "security guards" my grandmother had told me about: elderly men, many of them veterans, who drove around in golf carts looking for trouble. They carried pepper spray and big black walkie-talkies in case they had to call the sheriff for backup. Usually, they just kept an eye on vacated homes or kicked a few trespassers out of the pool. The month before, though, they'd discovered one of Grandma's neighbors splayed across her driveway, dead from the heat.

I slipped into the shallow end of the pool with hardly a wince. The water was kept exactly at medically recommended temperatures; there was no gasp, no shock to the heart. I swam a few laps, then paused in the middle of the water. I was the only one in the pool—no other teenagers or children, no splashing or diving or chicken fights. No insect-and-goober slicks. Grandma had explained at breakfast that young people and families were welcome to live in Green Valley, just not in the gated neighborhoods that dominated the interior of the community. No one under eighteen could reside in Pueblo Estates, and no one under fifty-five could buy a home there. Grandma had told me a story about a middle-aged couple who'd moved into one of the parks several years ago. When the woman unexpectedly became pregnant, neighbors held a shower, sent cards and flowers, then politely asked them to leave.

"Oh well," Grandma sighed, "they knew the rules."

I gazed at the distant, isolated condos where the banished young people lived, and at the scruffy foothills rising above them, becoming mountains. It seemed almost perverse to be swimming in the desert, but that was one of the few promises of the place that had been kept. The winter before my grandparents left for Green Valley, while driving me home from the maintenance garage, Grandpa Andy had talked on and on about how it was sunny all year round in Arizona and how you could swim and play golf in December. "You'll come down and I promise you'll love it," he said, pausing to suck on a lemon rind. Part of me looked forward to that, but mostly it made me sad, all that talk of the desert. It was as if, in some mysterious way, he was already gone. I peered out the frosted window at the warm living-room lights and sparkling snow and the soft steam rising off the houses and wondered why he wanted to leave. It was so beautiful, I thought then, and we were together. Grandpa took another lemon rind off the seat, placed it in his mouth, and flashed me a crazy, sun-yellow smile that made me laugh. Later, I told Mom about that smile, and she pursed her lips and got quiet. She had an angry conversation with him about it at some point—the lemon rinds, the driving with me in the truck—and the Arizona launch date was suddenly moved up. I remember Grandma Kathryn crying, all of us crying, as they dumped their furniture into our garage—she didn't want to leave so soon, she said. But Grandpa's mind was set. All that work wasn't enough to erase some mistakes. There had to be the leaving.

Out in the actual desert, while I swam, the sun beat shadows out of a thousand saguaro cacti. What is it they say—each arm takes sixty years to grow? Many saguaros were sporting five, even six arms, which made me wonder if their cacti grandparents had hailed the Conquistador Francisco Vásquez de Coronado when he arrived there over four hundred years ago. I'd read about it in the "Exciting History of Green Valley!" booklet Grandma had sent me. Coronado had been searching for Cibola, the legendary city of gold. What he actually found must've been a big disappointment: leagues of bone-dry soil, ancient ironwood, devil's fingers, the million twisted specters of saguaro. The one place, perhaps, that could match and engulf his inexhaustible desire for immortality. Even I could sense it, the humbling immensity of time. Death—the Jesuit who boils in his dark robe, the Pima woman murdered by soldiers in her sleep, the stillborn child—is nothing there. We are nothing. The desert is all there is, vast and invincible. Coronado quickly moved on, as far north as the prairies of future Kansas, leaving the Sonora to what must have seemed its proper inhabitants: the old, the penitent, and the dead.

Inside the giant white Lincoln, Grandma scolded me for not talking more with Grandpa, for spending all that time at the pool. "He woke up and wondered where you were," she said. I didn't respond, because I suspected this wasn't true, that it had been she who'd wondered. We were alone together on Interstate 19, which levitated and rippled over the desert, heading toward the Titan Missile Museum just north of Green Valley. If there was time afterward, we planned to catch a guided nature tour of Sabino Canyon—Esther's painting of that lush desert place hung in my Iowa City apartment, to remind me that such places existed. For Grandma, this day trip was part of an ongoing effort to encourage my interest in science. She was overjoyed I was taking premedicine courses in college. "You'll heal so many people," she'd told me, "maybe even cure cancer or crippled people, if you put your mind to it. You have a wonderful brain, John, far more advanced than other kids your age." What Grandma didn't know was that, halfway through my junior year, I was about to drop premedicine and focus full time on literature and writing. I'd given it a decent effort, and was still working as a nursing assistant in a children's hospital, but I saw the end coming. As much as I wanted to think otherwise, I'd hate to disappoint her.

Grandma didn't like to talk about her own youth—no immigrant songs on the porch or cherished recipes or annual visits to the family farmstead. What I'd managed to piece together, at that point, was that she'd been an eldest child and had a younger sister, Virginia. Her father, a factory worker and part-time professional baseball player in Chicago, had abandoned the family when Grandma was a child, but still old enough to remember. Her mother, Nina, had moved back to Iowa and married twice again (one husband may have been murdered in the basement of their Fort Dodge apartment building). She'd sent Kathryn and Virginia to live on her parents' farm in nearby Lehigh and saw them on the weekends. In high school, Kathryn had loved the Romantic poets and Latin and wanted to attend university, but her grandfather had sent Virginia instead because, according to Grandma, he thought she was prettier and smarter. So she married a handsome, hardworking, but poor son of Swedish immigrants and settled into a life that, like the life before, seemed to strand her just shy of happiness.

Except when it came to me. Shortly after my "miraculous" birth, Grandma had decided that every month she'd buy me a "first"—my first teddy bear, my first rattle, my first stroller, and, when I was a little older, my first tricycle, my first set of golf clubs, my first switchblade comb. If my father complained, she'd complain louder, perhaps in front of their friends: "Well,

John, I *would* buy you that big expensive thing you want, but I wouldn't want to hurt your dad's *feelings*." The one time she didn't get her way was when she tried to buy me a Shetland pony to keep in our front yard, and that's because the city wouldn't allow it. The gifts continued to flow, nonetheless, and they were still flowing—a TV for my apartment, a new stereo, a leather bomber's jacket. To others she often seemed difficult and critical, which she was, laying into my mother about her weight or my sisters about their bad manners and unlucky hair or my father about his lack of ambition. When we sat and talked about Grandma, my family and I, wondering if anything would ever satisfy her, the silent and perplexing answer was that, well, I did.

I suspected that was the real reason no one volunteered to join us on that educational trip: I was expected to earn all those extra gifts by allowing them more time to have fun. The same thing had happened during our last visit to Arizona, six years ago. While my sisters lounged at the pool or went shopping with Mom in Tucson, Grandma and I spent the afternoons driving in front of suburban mansions—"You could live there someday, Dr. Price"—and touring historical sites, like the Mission San Xavier del Bac. I was reminded of that visit by the mission's white bell tower, which I could see just beyond the edge of the highway. I was fourteen when I first visited the "Dove of the Desert," and though over two hundred years old, it had seemed in sympathy with my adolescent spirit: awkward, out of place, passionately symbolic. The burnt brick facade, for instance, with its outside edges spiraling inward toward the royal lions of Castile and, nearly hidden within the western spiral, a small stone mouse. Facing it, within the eastern spiral, was a crouching cat. When the cat catches the mouse, local legend says, the world will end.

"Do you still pray for your grandfather?" Grandma asked, perhaps also noticing the mission tower. "If you can't talk to him, I hope you can at least pray for him." I pretended I didn't hear this, fearing another lecture on how she came from a time when people took care of their own (with the exception of her father, I was always tempted to reply). She had, in fact, taken care of someone in each generation of her family, starting with her own grandmother, Josephine, cooking meals for her during the first years of Alzheimer's and then, when she had to be admitted to the county home, staging ice cream socials for her and her decimated floormates. She'd cared for Billy, her sister Virginia's boy—only three years old when he died from Hirschsprung's disease—massaging his distended belly, quieting his nightly screams by singing and holding his face up to the moon. She'd moved to Seattle for a few months, leaving Grandpa behind, to nurse her mother through the final tortures of cancer. She'd even tried to help her sister—the prettier, smarter one—fight her addiction to pain killers, though Virginia would eventually commit suicide in British Columbia.

As for Grandpa, she'd raged against his drinking for most of their married life and then, in Arizona, dealt with the consequences, nursing his stroked-out body, measuring foods and carefully laying out vitamins and scheduling doctor appointments. It was easy to see sometimes why happiness had been so elusive. But Grandma probably would've insisted her story was not about being unhappy; it was about faith. Through it all she'd come to believe that God was alive and at work in her world, giving strength when she prayed for it, and mercy and healing. Just look at Grandpa Andy—the doctors claimed he'd never walk again. When you do the right thing, like praying and taking care of the sick, you call God's grace into your life. You are rewarded.

I wasn't as sure. Despite her prayers, nothing in the desert seemed to have turned out as it should for my grandparents. My prayers didn't seem capable of taking root there, either. Six years before, inside the San Xavier Mission, I'd stood beside the effigy of its patron saint, the Apostle of the Indies, reclining in the west sanctuary with hundreds of silver milagros—feet, hands, eyes, hearts—pinned to his shroud. Beneath his plaster head there was a nest of paper notes on which the Tohono O'odham and Pima devout had written their questions, prayers, and confessions. I watched a few of them bowing and crossing themselves before the effigy, lifting the head to insert another scrap of paper. It had been a long time since I'd prayed, but while studying the cracked face and glued-on hair—thin and wispy like my grandfather's—I must've sensed some promise. I pulled a gum wrapper out of my pocket, grabbed a pencil from the guest book, and scribbled out a prayer for his frozen legs. After lifting the head, which was surprisingly heavy, I placed the wrapper underneath. I stood there, waiting, until Grandma slipped her hand inside my arm.

"Was that for your grandfather?" she asked, already knowing the answer.

We turned onto the dirt road that led to the Titan Missile Museum. The complex was set low and flat, with a few communication towers extending like robot fingers into the air. They were all we could see for several miles until, rounding a desert swell, the white cap of the silo became starkly visible. After parking the Lincoln, we walked inside the once electrified gates where pieces of a missile were scattered—a fuselage, a reentry vehicle—in front of which families were being photographed. Grandma saw me staring at them and assumed I was studying the science. "You could invent something like that," she said. "You have such a wonderful brain, John—I've always told you that." She warned me not to waste my God-given talents (as I think she suspected I was about to), and to remember how Grandpa had never had my opportunities, how he'd always wanted to go to college but had ended up shoveling coal and chasing bad wires for the city and then, after all that hard work, suffering a stroke. She hasn't a clue, I thought.

Still, there was this tenderness. She hung onto my arm as I escorted her into the information center and through the gift shop, where peppy seniors sold coffee cups and T-shirts decorated with images of the missile blasting out of its silo, as vivid as any of my comic books. We entered a small, crowded theater and managed to find a couple of folding chairs near the front, just as the lights were dimming. The film's narrator explained that this particular Titan missile complex, called the Copper Penny, had been installed in 1963 as part of a larger nuclear arsenal in the Tucson area. The retirement community of Green Valley, unofficially founded in 1967, had quickly blossomed around the site. The Copper Penny had been taken off alert in

1982, but before it could be completely deactivated and destroyed, Green Valley civic leaders—meaning, I supposed, aging retirees like my grandparents—had lobbied the U.S. Air Force, the Department of Defense, and the Soviet government to preserve the site as a significant part of local and world "history." Permission was eventually granted, but not until the missile was dragged out of its silo and photographed by Soviet satellites for six weeks. The site was then converted into a museum, the only one of its kind in the world.

When the film ended our tour leader, Gene, a retired U.S. Air Force officer and Green Valley resident, distributed hard hats and led us to a secret underground entrance at the far corner of the compound. Near the door was a sign—*Beware of Rattlesnakes!*—placed there when the area was largely uninhabited desert. Gene assured us that now, thanks to tens of thousands of tourists, there was little chance of encountering snakes or lizards or dangerous animals of any kind.

We descended several flights to the underground facilities. Grandma grabbed my arm tighter, carefully choosing her steps, holding up a line of people. Some of them exhaled loudly. After negotiating a maze of hallways, Gene led us through a three-ton blast door and into the dim silo. The crowd pushed forward. On the other side of the observation glass was the Titan missile, safely tucked into its launch cylinder. I squirmed my way to the front and squashed my cheek against the glass. What I saw, at first, was a blurry reflection of our faces on the weapon's shiny surface. I twisted my neck, but couldn't see the top of the missile; it was that huge—110 feet long, 10 feet in diameter, and 170 tons. In its prime, it could have destroyed a city the size of

Tucson. Gene told us all kinds of real-life horror stories about crew members getting vaporized by accidental explosions or squashed by folding maintenance ramps or burned alive inside leaky chemical suits—the kind of stories I somehow wanted to hear inside such a sterile, tight-fisted place. There beneath the surface, Gene said, we could withstand a direct nuclear hit from the enemy and not even spill our Cokes.

"Yeah," some guy snickered, "but what about the outside?"

Gene stiffened: "What about it?"

I retreated to the edge of the crowd. "You left me behind," Grandma scolded, returning her hand to my arm. "A young gentleman never leaves his lady companion." I apologized as Gene led us back through the blast doors and into the control center. It was cramped but well organized, walled with file-cabinet computers, switch boxes, graph machines, and black surveillance screens. Almost everything was stainless steel or concrete and painted hospital green. There were a few metal chairs at each station, the same kind found at church picnics. Gene explained the function of each station: one for communications, one for technical maintenance, one for the Doppler radar screens (or "tipsies"), and two for activating the booster rockets. If a launch order had actually arrived, the officers would not have been informed of the missile's destination, only that it was leaving. They would've been required, simply, to turn two keys simultaneously, as if opening a suitcase. One hyperbolic fuel would meet the other, ignite, and send the missile miles into the sky and then down again.

I looked around the room. How small and unselfconscious it was, gray wires running neatly above our heads, metal surfaces wiped clean. There were no questions there. Not like the desert or the sanctuary at San Xavier, where every surface was heavy with symbol and story, where to walk from door to altar was to ascend the cross of Christ. But story may have informed this place, as well. I tried to recall what I'd learned about the Titans in my Classical and Biblical Lit class the previous semester, one of the courses I'd been telling Grandpa about when he'd dozed off that morning. There was Chaos, who gave birth to Heaven and Earth, who were then overthrown by their children, the Titans, who were then overthrown by their children, the Olympians—Zeus, Hera, Poseidon, and the rest. I wondered which of the Titans, if any, had inspired the name for the missile. Was it Atlas, bearing the weight of the universe on his shoulders; or Prometheus, who gave fire to humans and as eternal punishment was strapped alive to a rock, where a vulture feasted daily on his liver? Maybe it referred to Kronos, Father Time. In one story, Kronos ruled over a golden age of innocence and purity, while in another he was a savage monster, so jealous of his children, so paranoid they would usurp him, he devoured them whole. Or did the name just refer to the missile's size?

Grandma elbowed me in the ribs: "Why don't you go up there?" Gene had apparently asked for volunteers. "Go on," she said, giving me another jab, "you might just learn something." I ignored her, but then she called out—"Over here!"—and everyone turned to see her pointing at me. Gene hesitated, looked around, then gestured for me to come forward. I reluctantly made my way through the crowd and he assigned me to one of the launch consuls. To my left, occupying the other consuls, were a boy and a girl, both around nine or ten years old. They stared at me. No wonder Gene had hesitated—this was a child's exercise—and I thought I saw a few eyes rolling in the audience. Grandma was beaming, as if this was my fourth-grade piano recital.

Gene placed a tape of a simulated launch sequence into a portable cassette player. "Just follow along," he said. A loud, static voice announced the code word for launch clearance. Gene instructed the boy at the communications consul to punch the destination code into his panel. The girl and I removed our keys from the lockbox and inserted them into the designated slots. On Gene's count of three, we turned our keys.

"Launch is now a go-go," he said.

The crowd was silent. Some were staring at the floor, while others looked blankly at Gene and at us, as if they'd missed something or expected more to be said. But Gene was done talking. The boy and girl rejoined the crowd; everyone began moving slowly through the blast doors. I stayed in my seat, until I felt Grandma's arms around my neck.

"I'm so proud of you," she said.

"What?" I responded, harshly. "How can you say that? That was terrible."

She thought I was referring to the missile.

"No, no," she said. "It doesn't have to be terrible. That's why we have faith in Jesus. Don't you ever forget that, John. Not ever." Her voice was loud enough to make several people stop and turn around. My anger dissipated. I stood and escorted her to the surface.

In the museum parking lot, Grandma said she was tired and asked me to drive her home; we would not be going to Sabino Canyon or anywhere else.

"Mexico?" she asked, gazing out the window as we moved down the highway.

"What?"

"Maybe we can go to Mexico tomorrow. I haven't been there in years."

"Maybe," I shrugged. The last time I'd visited the border at Nogales, when I was fourteen, Grandma had bought me a chess set carved from local stone and polished to a bright sparkle. While leaving the store, I'd nearly tripped over a blind woman sitting on the curb, begging for change. She held a painting of the Sacred Heart while, beside her, two children lapped a puddle of spilled Coke off the concrete.

"Well, if you don't want to go to Mexico with me," she snapped, "then promise you'll at least spend some time with your grandfather. You can't imagine how happy that would make him, John. He's been so looking forward to your visit."

I promised, but at the time I was more worried about her happiness. About the day, and it would be coming soon, when she realized she couldn't save him. That I couldn't save him either, or her—not as a doctor or as a rocket scientist or as a gift from God. Not even as a grandson who loved them.

Later that day, I sat in my grandparents' driveway and watched the sunset unfold, rose and vermilion, across the Santa Ritas. In the foothills, the shadows of the saguaros blurred. Living-room lights caressed the rock gardens and wide streets of Pueblo Estates, while the scent of popcorn and the sound of wind chimes floated in the air. Time softened, the imagination reclined—it appeared the cat would, at least for that evening, be kept from the mouse. On the small putting green near the patio, Grandpa was tapping nine holes with Mom and Allyson, who had recently turned ten years old. Although he was leaning on his walker, his legs appeared remarkably straight. I wasn't spending time with him at the moment and he didn't seem to mind. Grandma was standing in the doorway, handing apricots to Carrie Anne and Susan, who bit into them, juice running down their chins. She didn't know it yet, but she'd already forgiven me for not going to medical school. My father was sitting in a lawn chair, reading a book. He wasn't making any special effort to converse with his in-laws, and yet he was there, spending his one week of vacation with them and with us. We were all there, which reminded me of another legend I'd learned at the San Xavier Mission. To offer a prayer, you must first lift the head of the saint. To lift the head, they say, is to be already good at heart.

A blaze of aureate erupted in the saddle of the mountains, and the desert seemed to come alive. The wind picked up, scattering the leaves of the palo verde. A quail cried. A tiny lizard scurried in front of me, paused, then darted beneath the barrel cactus. I pointed at it, but the lizard was gone and I was left with my arm extending into space. I felt foolish, until I noticed my grandmother watching me and I saw the moment through her eyes.

His finger on the world, once again. As it should be.

NIGHT RHYTHMS

⬥

I leave Dean's bedside to make 2 A.M. rounds. The in-patient unit at the children's hospital is dim and silent except for a metallic hum that can be heard, just barely, in the air. I am in my nursing assistant uniform, white, except for the splotch of creamed ham I spilled on the leg during a now distant daytime feeding. There are eleven patients, all children, the oldest nineteen, only a couple of years younger than me. They're all disabled—cerebral palsy, muscular dystrophy, failure-to-thrive. But that is during the day. They're asleep now, free from their daytime gnawing and spasms.

My assignment tonight is to go from one room to the next, checking diapers and catheters. This round there are not many to check. So I just listen to their breathing, and if it is too silent, I place my hand on their rib cage, gently, to feel the measure of their sleep. I'm glad it's not the designated hour to reposition them, to wake them, interrupt, and if they've had surgery, to cause them pain. That time is two hours away. For now, I can just watch and feel for their breath, celebrating the trail of drool for what it means: peace. Sleep the elixir. I am extra quiet.

I return to Dean's bedside. There is a blue swelling near his ankle where, earlier in the evening, Dr. Van Skeldt tried to insert an IV needle, again and again. It was clear then that we would have to transfer him to the main hospital, where they are better equipped to deal with him. Dr. Van Skeldt has left to make arrangements. The night nurse enters, support hose rubbing and swishing, to register what vitals she can. "Why did he have to bring him here?" she says. "He knew we wouldn't be able to take care of him. He knew that." But the care facility won't take him back, I remind her. Maybe this is the only place he has.

"Well, I don't know about that."

She's right, in a way—our small unit isn't equipped to handle a patient like Dean. Yet here he is. Dean won't live much longer. He has severe cerebral palsy, which means he choked during birth, which means the rhythm of the contractions were wrong. His lungs opened too soon. He has lived seventeen years, barely. I pull up a chair and sit at his bedside. I watch his rib cage extend then collapse: up . . . down . . . up, up, up . . . down. His lips, dry, are collecting a thin film of mucus, which I wipe away with a damp cloth. His auburn hair shines with nearly three days' oil. He is so emaciated that when the fluorescent bulb, like an alien sun, casts blue upon his twisted limbs, it sends shadows in odd places, unexpected: pelvis, upper lip, ribs . . .

An hour later I leave Dean's bedside to clean the sunroom. This is the children's playroom, now empty. Around me the carpet, the plastic chairs and tables are covered with the daytime patterns of childhood, lingering. Toys and pieces of toys lie here and there, always everywhere, weaving messy spirals and rhythms and textures. Yellow, red, blue. Minihouses, Ken heads, Fisher-Price farms, hollow plastic bulbs—some together, some not. I pick them up, one by one, and put them in their designated places. During my two years here, I've often worked the evening shift, just after supper, when the sunroom is full of children, of wet hair and pajamas; movement and noise; tricycles, storybooks, gossip; house, cops, robbers; tossing, chasing, shouting. *John, John, John,* they called from all corners, all sides. The supervisor's big butt, Dan's booger, Kara's farts. Faster and faster, the kinetic energy of their play seemed to raise the small hairs on my neck and arms . . . and so I'd forget. On the mat, near the television, were the other patients like Dean. Motionless, except for the occasional rocking from seizures. Movement would flurry about them, balls accidentally bouncing off their heads as we nursing assistants played with the other children, all of us believing, hoping, that because these patients lay quiet, just breathing and rocking, they were pacified. Bright colors spinning around us, we would tuck them and their gnarled fingers into the far corners of our minds.

But here on the night shift, I remember.

I return to Dean's bedside. His steamer is stuttering. I lift the top to add a pint of distilled water and, as it flows, I think of my brother. He was buried fifteen years ago in soft blue terry-cloth pajamas at a funeral I wasn't allowed to attend. Sometimes I dream about that funeral, but not very often anymore. In fact, I haven't thought of James much at all recently. But tonight is different. From Dean's window I can see through the shadow-leafed locusts to a distant intersection where the traffic lights are changing by themselves. Green, yellow, red, again and again . . . no one is awake to heed them except me. I'm on the night shift, and feel as if I'm privy to the secrets of day existence, privy to the secret knowledge that pedestrian buttons on traffic lights are an illusion. There is no real control. The lights change according to timers, predetermined rhythms that go unnoticed during the day like the regular seizures of children who lie on playroom mats. But at night I can see them changing while others sleep.

It seems unimportant, unless you realize that just over the curve of the earth, beyond this sleep time, are daytime lands and cities where people and machines are pounding and cars jam cloverleaf junctions and planes are landing and emerging through thunder. People barbecuing, starving, mowing lawns, riding camels or tugboats or the backs of lovers in pounding, ceaseless, pulsating patterns and rhythms that blend into palimpsestic nonsense until just once—*just once*—the synchronization goes bad and you find yourself standing near a Dean and counting the number of times his rib cage rises, watching as a doctor jabs and jabs and jabs an IV needle into the tender flesh of his foot in the hope of finding a vessel with a pulse. Or you find yourself a woman in labor, in an empty hospital room in April, whimpering as you feel the kicking against your abdomen dwindle to nothing. Or you find yourself a father standing outside your remaining son's doorway, the night before Easter, letting the candies drop from your hand and onto the carpet, one by one by one. Or, at seven, you find yourself alone in a closet, quietly tearing out fistfuls of your hair because the baby died and, somehow, you know it's your fault.

Dean coughs, just a little, and returns to the wet labor of his breathing. Softly, carefully, I slip my thumb into his small velvet palm and caress the top of his hand with my index finger. I don't know if he notices, but I feel the need. The need to shout him on, to set the pace of his life stream, to fill arteries and lungs and heart. On my caress he'll live out the evening, keep breathing, stop choking, become born. But who is this boy to me, anyway? Maybe this is another family legacy, to care for the one most in need, inherited from my nurse mother, from my faithful, vigilant grandmother. James was lost during the night shift, when a nurse left my mother in a room alone, unmonitored. Maybe Dean is who James would've been if he'd lived, a good portion of his brain suffocated. Maybe I've been trying all along to set things right. Maybe I'm just tired.

I don't know. I don't know why I'm sitting here, why, out of the hundreds of children I've assisted in this place, some terminally ill, I should feel the need to especially comfort this boy on this night. I just do. So I sit and caress and listen, beneath the hum of machines, for the breath of life, and the secret rhythms of compassion.

Too quickly, Dr. Van Skeldt enters the room, and the night nurse is with him. They have brought a cart for the transfer. He has decided not to use motor transport and I wonder why. Why push him when you could drive him the short, bumpy distance to Main? I don't know a lot about Dr. Van Skeldt except that he arrived from Boston, is divorced, and lives alone, no children. Usually, he walks around the halls with a grave brow, checking a file or two, rarely going too far out of his way for patient or staff. He's considered rather cold.

But his relationship with Dean has been a mystery to everyone. Among staff, Dean is referred to as Dr. Van Skeldt's

personal "project." He checks in on Dean every evening, meeting with staff in the process, courteously begging favors from
us for his care: *Could you put a pillow there, please?* And tonight,
when Dean whimpered as the needle kept missing its mark, I
thought I read, on Dr. Van Skeldt's brow, a wrinkle of pain. He
has had to move Dean from one facility to the next, trying to
find a place willing to take care of him until he dies. Now we
can't keep him either.

Dr. Van Skeldt takes the two far ends of Dean's bed sheet
and I grab the near. Slowly we lift him, with the nurse's help,
from his bed to the cart. Dean's eyes are moving back and forth,
his breath stretching toward a whimper. He is crying, I can tell,
and frightened. Slowly we start to move—Dr. Van Skeldt in
front, me in back—past the nurse, out the door and onto the
cracked sidewalk that leads to the main hospital. It is an Iowa
summer at night. A mist has risen out of the river valley to engulf the grassy courtyard, the lone linden tree, soaking the fur of
rabbits as they nibble, calling witness to the indisputable fact
that the earth itself breathes. There is the smell of damp soil, the
faint hint of mock orange blossoms. We stop moving.

"Isn't that pretty?" Dr. Van Skeldt says to himself, or maybe
to Dean. "I caught that scent earlier. I was hoping it would still
be here for us. It reminds me of California when I was a boy.
The smell of those blossoms filled the air. My mother used to
say that if you breathed too much of it you would faint away or
lose your socks or something. That's what she used to say then.
There it is again . . . isn't that something?"

Dr. Van Skeldt pauses, touches Dean's shoulder. He checks
the IV pole. And we move on, toward the bright fluorescent
lights of Main.

PART TWO

New Lands

LOVE MOUNTAIN

"Come down from there, dammit!"

It's our honeymoon and I awaken, as if from a trance, to find myself clinging to the side of a cliff in the Sawtooth wilderness of Idaho. The situation is new to me—being married, clinging to the side of a mountain—and, at the moment, unexpectedly precarious: a surprise visit from a loose pebble or a curious pika will put an end to it all. This explains, perhaps, the insistence in Steph's voice. I can see her, maybe a hundred feet below, standing on one of numerous jagged rocks, shouting, but I ignore her, preoccupied with the withering strength in my feet and fingertips and with the undeniable fact that *this is her fault.* How many times did I tell her that flatlanders like me should not be allowed to wander the higher elevations of our country? How many times did I point out that Idaho militia groups are stocked with ex-pat Midwesterners? How many times did I mention, in passing, that the Donners were from Illinois? Countless numbers of my kind have thrown themselves with little forethought into the western wilderness, only to become disoriented and lost and, if they're lucky, airlifted to safety like dew-eyed moose calves on *Mutual of Omaha's Wild Kingdom*. If they're unlucky—and many have been—they die, die by the bushel inside the hidden cracks of canyons or beneath the smothering blanket of an avalanche or, like me, on a slippery cliff they can't remember climbing or why. Steph had read about these unlucky people in the paper, she'd witnessed my own erratic behavior in the mountains, and yet, somehow, while photographing wildflowers, she'd allowed me to wander off alone.

If I survive, I'll confront her about this, but I suspect I won't survive. I suspect our relationship is about to end very much the way it began: a man staring across space, falling.

I saw her across a room. No one should be allowed to start a love story with this line, but I have breathed the thin air and am oblivious. It was a college cafeteria, about four years earlier, when I was twenty-one. I was attending my sister Carrie Anne's graduation from Cottey College, a private two-year women's school in Missouri, founded by PEO, an international women's organization. No man was allowed into their organization or the school.

So I had that going for me. In the cafeteria, I noticed Steph right away, struck by her beauty, her long dark hair, and by the massive, unapologetic mountain of food on her plate—my life felt in need of that kind of generosity. Earlier that same week, in Iowa City, I'd graduated with my BA in Religion. After finally dropping premedicine—a move that still felt vaguely like betrayal—I'd taken the advice of one of my English professors and applied, at the last possible moment, to the graduate literature and writing program at the University of Iowa. I'd intended to go someplace else after graduating, but there'd been no time to think it through and apply to other schools. And with my relative lack of coursework and faculty connections, my abysmal Graduate Record Exam scores, I wasn't sure anyplace else would've taken me. So there I was again, returning to the same university in the fall, with no clear purpose, no training, no scholarship or teaching assistantship to help me afford tuition, nothing but my nursing assistant job at the hospital—a heavy relic of past dreams and reasons that, like the place itself, I couldn't seem to shake.

Returning to Fort Dodge from Cottey, I interrogated my sister and found out Steph was from Idaho, that she was kind, studious, outdoorsy, and listened to Gordon Lightfoot. "She conducted a bird funeral," Carrie Anne added. *A bird funeral?* "Yes, a funeral for a bird, a robin. She invited her friends, built a little cardboard coffin, and buried it in the middle of the quad. A little weird if you ask me."

I immediately crafted a letter of introduction, perhaps my first serious foray into creative nonfiction, in which I foregrounded my acceptance to graduate school, my love of hiking and songbirds, and my passion (until then, unrealized) for Gordon Lightfoot. The letter eventually reached Steph at Camp Sawtooth, a church camp where she'd spent most of her summers since late childhood and now worked as a cook. The camp is part of a huge wilderness area in central Idaho, hundreds of square miles of forests and rivers and mountain peaks, many over ten thousand feet—yet another isolated place with very few men. Steph found my letter intriguing; her roommate found it suspicious. What are the chances, she remarked, that the only two Gordon Lightfoot fans from our generation would find each other? She discouraged Steph from responding, but there were ulterior motives. The roommate was trying to rekindle a romance between Steph and her fiancé's buddy, the wealthy heir of a cement-mixing company. Mr. Concrete had his own private plane, and for their first date he had picked Steph up at her Cottey dormitory and flown her to Springfield, Missouri, to do the town, such as it is. The plane ride was impressive, Steph later told me, but he went overboard when he bought her a rose at the shopping mall. That was too much, she said, too contrived, too scripted. But my letter, well, that was another thing altogether.

Steph wrote back, and during the next year there were more letters and phone calls and then visits to her school in Missouri and mine in Iowa. We liked to spend time at a state park near Iowa City, on the Cedar River, where I demonstrated my outdoorsiness by repeatedly leading her into thickets of sticktights, nettle, and poison oak. Once, on a can-littered sandbar, I dug out a river mussel and handed it to her. She touched the soft pale "foot" extending from the shell and it snapped shut, squirting water on her. I told her she could count the rings on that shell to know how old it was, like a tree. She was impressed, I think.

Later that summer, Steph's father, Gary, who'd been raised in Iowa and regularly returned to visit his parents, offered to drive us both to Idaho, where I could meet the rest of the family. As we crossed Nebraska, Gary impressed me as a kind and generous man, repeatedly playing a cassette of Gordon Lightfoot tunes, who he'd heard was a favorite of mine. But when we entered Wyoming, he popped in Frankie Laine—*Bullet in my shoulder! Blood runnin' down my vest! Twenty in the posse, and they're never going to let me rest!*—and whistled out the window: "Gosh, I just love this country! Makes me feel *alive!*" The Volare veered onto an empty road and accelerated across a vast sageland flat that extended, like a dying breath, to the foothills of craggy, snowless mountains. There were vultures. I became anxious—here was another ex-Midwesterner blasting off into the territories—until we stopped for a picnic along the banks of the Wind River. We sat in the trembling shade of a cottonwood, admiring the red rock bluffs. Steph waded across the shallow water to sit on a large rock, in the sun. As I watched her in that direct, nearly unbearable light, it became one of those moments you sometimes experience as a child, when the eyes fix and the corners of sight fold in and you feel on the edge of a promising dream. I suspect that near the beginning of every meaningful love there is a place, a particular place, and I knew it even then. My mind opened to the western space that seemed to enfold and define her—the new air, the rough and magnificent possibilities of wind, water, and time. The possibilities.

Steph and I got engaged that Christmas and she moved to Iowa. For the first six months, to earn in-state tuition, she lived with her grandparents in Tama, sixty miles away, working at a local fast-food restaurant. The situation was once again to my advantage—she saw very few men besides her grandpa Lloyd and pimply coworkers, who reeked of fry grease—but it took a toll on her. She loved her grandparents, and Tama was a familiar place, but it wasn't home. The prairie winter (even without the prairie) was dark and snowy and bitterly cold, and she spent much of it huddled against the register with a blanket over her head. I joined her on the weekends, making guilty promises about what we'd do when the warm weather returned and beyond. We would travel to Idaho, of course, and after earning my doctorate, I'd land a teaching job in the mountain west and we'd live there forever. She said I shouldn't make promises I couldn't keep. I was offended—*I love the West, the mountains, as much as you do!*—but she said she meant the part about getting a job.

That summer, as promised, we traveled to Idaho. Caldwell, Steph's hometown, is a small college town perched on the edge of the Great Basin desert, which is definitely not cold. Even so, it reminded me of Iowa. The Treasure Valley, including the Caldwell area, is a heavily irrigated, agricultural, and urban place. There's lots of corn. It has its secret wonders, though, such as the way the air smells of sage and mint after a rainfall. During our first visit, Steph had taken me to see the lacy waterfalls and hidden pools at nearby Jump Creek Canyon in the Owyhee Mountains, a range named for a group of touring Hawaiians who'd vanished there in the 1800s—perhaps another people who shouldn't be allowed to roam the western elevations.

This time, Steph insisted on taking me to Camp Sawtooth—her "spiritual home," as she called it. Now that we were engaged, she wanted me to finally see it, to experience its beauty and significance.

The trip from Caldwell to camp was one long ascent from the sage-smoked desert to the forests and mountains. Gradually, a breeze that smelled of hot onions and dirt began to hint of pinesap and river-wet grass. Shade blanketed the interior and I gazed up to see steep, aspen-dusted slopes with granite

outcroppings, and an occasional white slice of Soldier Mountain. Steph proclaimed it "another world," and ecologically
speaking it is, but for me it was disorienting and scary. The
proximity of rock walls and trees seemed to amplify our speed,
and once, when a logging truck came barreling around a blind
curve, I screamed.

At the edge of Camp Sawtooth, the trees fell back and we
entered a wide meadow, dotted with flowers. A cluster of log
buildings was set near the rushing South Fork of the Boise
River. Steph's sister, Amy, a counselor there, greeted us at the
lodge. She asked what I thought about the Sawtooths, and
though still nauseous, I replied that I already felt deeply connected and couldn't wait to go on a hike. Steph looked at me side-
ways, perhaps recalling the scream, but an unfamiliar, furious
resolve had begun to infect my brain, like a fever. When Amy
suggested following the camp trail to a nearby ridgeline, I insisted
I wanted to get off the beaten path, I wanted to experience something wilder, I wanted to see what this country was all about—I
hadn't come all the way up here to follow some kiddy trail . . .

"I get the picture," Amy interrupted. "How about Ross
Fork Lakes?"

Steph glared at her and said something about the truck being old, about how far it was and how high and how long it
would take—all day—to hike there and back.

"Sounds perfect!" I exclaimed.

The next morning we arose at daybreak, because I hadn't
slept. Her dad had loaned us his old pickup and I insisted on
driving. Steph agreed, which was the first of her many serious
miscalculations of my abilities. The road was basically two ruts

cutting through cement-hard dirt and boulders that shook us violently. I sped up.

"Take it easy!" she barked.

"I can handle the driving, thank you." I whistled as we sped along.

Miles later we stopped at what Steph called a "stream," but which was actually a river. They could usually drive across it, she said, but there'd been a lot of snowmelt. She suggested we return to camp and have Amy drive us across in the camp truck, which was bigger and more powerful. I responded by stomping on the accelerator. The truck hit the water and immediately stalled, the current nearly reaching the tops of the wheels. Steph was shouting at me, preparing to abandon ship, when three men emerged from the brush on the opposite shore. They sported unruly beards and greasy untucked flannels and were barely restraining a barking Doberman on a choke chain. One of the men waded out to the truck, asked if we were OK, and told me to pop the hood. He removed something from the engine, dried it with his shirt, and replaced it. The truck started; I put it in reverse and retreated to shore, where I yelled my thanks.

"Relax, buddy. Next time, don't take it so fast. Where're you from, anyway?"

"Iowa. How about you?"

"Michigan." And we left it at that.

Inside the wet, idling truck, Steph forced a smile and explained, in the singsong voice reserved for children, that we didn't have to go all the way back to camp. We could opt for the nearby Goat Lake trailhead. I told her I was reluctant to give up this glorious quest for something called Goat Lake, but if she'd decided to turn chicken on me, what choice was there? The hike to Goat Lake was, in fact, long and steep, and late in the afternoon we were surprised by a thundershower. I hadn't seen it coming, as I might've in the Midwest, and had left the rain gear in the truck. The temperature dropped dramatically; lightning flashed above the trees and ridgelines. Shivering, cramping, we finally reached the sapphire waters of Goat Lake, which I might've found pretty if we hadn't been on the verge of hypothermia. While discussing what to do next, besides lie down and die, we spotted a campfire through the thick pines. Two men in Gore-Tex rain suits—local teachers it turned out—were sitting on logs, drinking something hot. They could see we were nearly spasmodic and offered us a couple of blankets. Soon there was coffee and a schoolhouse lecture on being prepared. Steph nodded: "I'm from here and should've known better. It was stupid. This whole thing is stupid."

The fever lifted and I felt ashamed. Not only because the hike had been a disaster and that these men, and others, had had to save us from my idiocy. Mostly, I was ashamed that, after all of Steph's efforts and hopes, I felt no attraction to this harsh and supposedly beautiful country. Its significance was beyond my abilities. And yet Steph had been willing to leave it all for us—for me. Stupid, for sure.

During the next year in Iowa, between classes and work, we didn't see much of each other and the relationship suffered. We'd planned to get married the following summer, but called it off. Instead, we took another trip west. Neither of us said anything, but we knew it might be the last. This time we went to the Oregon coast—the cold, crashing waves of the Pacific, the delicate tidal pools, the Devil's Cauldron—an evasive, motion-burdened place that seemed to reflect our feelings for each other. During the drive back to Iowa, to pass the silent hours, Steph reread one of her favorite books, *The Stranger Beside Me*, a biography of serial killer Ted Bundy.

"Why the fascination?" I finally asked, refusing to hide the sarcasm. She shrugged.

"I guess it has something to do with the fact that Bundy was a westerner and that he drove through Caldwell, and also that you can know someone like the author knew Ted, but not really know him."

We then got into a heated debate over whether serial killers should be executed. Everyone has redeeming features, I argued, and from that point on, whenever I inquired about a town along the highway, about a local college or historical site, Steph would answer with the names of the women Ted had murdered in the area.

So it wasn't a joy ride. The long silences, the murders, the huge impersonal landscape—all of it made me feel out of place and vulnerable, like the injured crab we'd discovered in a tidal pool. It was only a matter of time.

Looking back, I marvel that anyone gets married. I'm still not sure why we went through with it, why we didn't end it after the trip to Oregon. Nothing really changed over the next year: I continued to be a less-than-ideal fiancé, and she continued to seem, at times, not to care if I lived or died. There was love between us, but what does that mean? What does it take at that age to convince anyone, especially yourself, that such a commitment is possible? That you are who you say and think you are? Can be?

Shortly before the wedding, a group of graduate school friends took me out to celebrate. We got drunk and, of course, ended up at a tattoo parlor. I perused the catalog, searching for an image to anchor my reeling emotions. There were few options among the dragons and skulls and big-busted Valkyries, so I searched my own woozy memory, arriving at the image of a bison. Not just any bison, but the big wild bull Steph and I had admired in front of the Tetons at dusk, during that first trip west with her father. It reminded me of that ideal time and also of the kind of husband I hoped to be: strong, brave, and *western*. There were no bison in the catalog, so I sketched one on a napkin, a brown blob the size of a quarter. Apparently, the tattoo artist didn't like me enough to improve the design. My friends squinted at the bloody splotch on my arm and wondered aloud what it was: A bear cub? A wombat? A fetus? Later, when I showed it to Steph, she squealed with laughter.

"Oh look, a puppy. How adorable!"

What does it take? I thought.

The wedding itself was beautiful and moving and I spent most of it in tears. Part of it was the pressure of taking our vows in front of all those friends and family, but mostly, I think I was just drained by the long emotional miles leading up to that deceptively simple moment. Steph was clear-eyed, a real ice queen, but I could tell she was drained, too. My tears would've been private if we hadn't videotaped the ceremony. The next day, while watching it at the gift reception, my brother-in-law Jake (whom Susan eventually had the sense to divorce) paused the video at the moment when, during my vows, my nose began to drip. He played it, then replayed it in slow motion—up, then down, then up again—while everyone hooted.

So I was greatly relieved when the festivities were over and we took off for the mountains. The staff at Camp Sawtooth had cleaned the mouse droppings and spiders out of an abandoned trailer, taped up a few streamers, and surprised us with a honeymoon suite. The next morning, for some reason, we decided to make another attempt at the Ross Fork Lakes. When we first discussed our honeymoon, Steph had suggested that we each choose a place to visit that was important to us as individuals. Her choice was obvious, but it took me a while to decide on Green Valley, Arizona, where Steph could meet my ailing grandfather. People were my primary landscape then—friends, family, self—and there seemed nothing incomplete about that. But as we were driving, slowly, across the mountain river where we'd once been stranded and then along the forest glens, the still pools, the magnificent peaks of her country, it hit me: *I'm taking my wife to a retirement community for our honeymoon.* Whatever else Green Valley was, it was not my spiritual home. I wasn't sure I had a spiritual home.

While we were walking the long trail toward the Ross Fork Lakes, Steph told me how she'd followed that same trail alone as a teenager and felt more completely herself, more at ease with her body, than ever before. She'd suffered from crushing self-doubt and anxiety, as I had, but there in the Sawtooths, at the Ross Fork Lakes, she'd stripped and swum without care and, on the pebbled shore, let the sun ignite her wet skin until she felt a part of all the beauty. Now she kept pausing to admire and caress a plant or tree or rock. "Look there," she'd say, "a shooting star," and kneel to smell the strong, sweet scent, the rose-colored petals bent back like a meteor in flight. And over there, that pond, which turned out to be a field of blue camas flowers. And over there, that unusual tree, its roots engulfing the boulder beneath, its bark twisted into a familiar face . . .

While she paused to take photos, I wandered ahead, following the thinning trail until I came upon a prospector's shack, a broken structure of weathered planks nearly hidden by the trees. I tried to imagine what the original occupant thought when he first arrived. He might get lost, become disillusioned, choose to flee—anyone might. So I continued walking, I don't know how far, until I reached an impassable cul-de-sac of granite cliffs towering over a field of jagged boulders. I studied the topographical map Amy had given us, which indicated the Ross Fork Lakes were directly over the ridgeline. If I'd looked at the map sooner, I would've seen that she'd marked a cutoff trail, nearly a mile back, which led around this dead end and up to the lakes. Steph might have reasonably assumed I'd read the map, tried to catch up to me on that other trail, and arrived at the lakes alone.

The fever returned. I started climbing one boulder after another, murmuring and cursing, bloodying my legs and arms as I tried not to fall into the dark chasms between rocks or into the large (too large) piles of scat. When I finally paused to gaze at the crenellated cliff tops, they appeared to be leaning forward, toppling, and I fell back against the rock. Strange sounds, whistles and low howls, emanated from the cracks and caves around me. The hiss of a wind I couldn't feel moved through and beyond, leaving me inside a stillness so complete I thought I could hear my own breath against the canyon walls, the blood pumping through my neck and temples . . .

That's all I remember until Steph's shouting awakened me halfway up the side of this cliff. There she is, a hundred feet and a million years below—a brown and yellow flower in a field of boulders. It came as a small revelation that she hadn't taken that other trail, the one her sister had marked on the map. She must've known I'd miss it. I'm sorry she's going to have to see me die, just when we were beginning to understand one another. But then the fear and regret make way for clarifying acceptance. There will be no helicopter rescue. There is only me and her and the rock. I take a minute to study the situation and can see there is a way down, but I need to be careful and I can't do it alone. I need her to keep shouting, which she does, letting me know if I'm about to miss a foothold or if I should move a little to the left or to the right. Somehow it works. I am moving, slowly, back down to the boulders, to the trail, which (I swear) we will immediately and without debate follow back to camp. I will not visit the Ross Fork Lakes that day, the place where Steph has lain with the wind, the rocks, the water.

And yet something has been forged here, a beginning. Who knows where it will lead? In the meantime, I'll try to get down from this cliff and recover my sanity and confront Steph. I'll tell her it was stupid to bring me here, stupid to let me wander off. I'll tell her it was stupid to marry me.

"I don't know," she'll say. "It was kind of a thrill seeing you up there. My husband, clinging to a cliff, risking his life to be with me."

And I'll think, *Is that all it takes?*

HIGH MAINTENANCE

I encountered the first illegal pet during a routine visit to fix a dripping faucet. Of course, being my first plumbing job as maintenance man for OK Apartments, it was anything but routine. The owners of the animal, college students like myself, had called that morning to report the leak and I'd spent the entire day preparing. I took notes from my five recently acquired fix-it books, bought additional tools, and chewed my fingernails into haggard, bloody nubs. It wasn't enough. When the fluffy blond tabby sauntered into their bathroom, I'd been working on the sink for over two hours, its grimy black parts scattered on the linoleum. To make matters worse, in order to disassemble this one faucet I'd had to cut off the water supply to half the complex. Unable to take a shower for their Friday dates or even flush their toilets, tenants were angrily calling Steph, who kept coming over to ask when I might be finished. On her fourth visit I was seriously tempted (for the first and only time in our marriage) to tell her to shut up and get me a beer.

After another half hour of futility, I stomped into the living room and called the previous maintenance man, Ted, on his cell phone. He said he'd be there in an hour. I broke the news of the delay to the tenants—two huge football-player types wearing soaked Hawkeye muscle shirts, one gold, the other gray. They'd just returned from the gym, sweat trickling off their prominent biceps and foreheads, and were probably desperate for a shower. I expected to get punched. Instead, they offered me the much-desired beer. As I took a long swig, they looked at each other, then lowered their heads.

"Are you going to tell the landlord about Ditka?" Gold finally asked, pointing at the cat rubbing against my ankles. He appeared to be on the verge of tears. "We don't have anywhere else to take him, except back to the shelter."

I should've seen it coming. During my interview for this job, Jerry, the co-owner of the apartment complex, had explained that my responsibilities included keeping an eye out for pets, a violation of the lease agreement. I was an unlikely candidate for any job that required fixing things—I'd only recently learned that cars require regular oil changes—but I'd been desperate. Steph and I were about to be married and we'd spent months trying to find an affordable apartment. Luckily, Jerry—an attractive man in his fifties, very white teeth—didn't test my mechanical knowledge. Instead, he asked me about my parents (he knew people in Fort Dodge), and was especially interested in our latest family dog, a Brittany spaniel. Jerry had a couple of Brittanys himself, he said. At the end of our conversation, to my surprise, he handed me the contract. For half off our rent, I would handle all maintenance duties for the twenty-four units in the complex. He added that if I needed any help, I could call Ted, my predecessor. Ted had resigned to dedicate more time to his mobile engine repair business, "Doctor High-way," but would still be living in the complex with his wife, Janet, who collected the rent, and their teenage daughter. Jerry emphasized, however, that I was to report all major mainte-nance issues, as well as any illegal pets, directly to him. We shook hands on it.

Now here I was, newly married and three hours into my first plumbing job, waiting for Ted to come to the rescue and being asked to decide the fate of someone's cat. I looked at the yellow beast, still rubbing against my shoe. I wasn't a fan of cats—I'd been bitten by one as a child—but at the moment, Ditka was probably the only resident of the complex that didn't want to kill me.

"No, I won't tell the landlord. Just try to keep him out of sight."

"Oh!" they exclaimed, massive shoulders slumping. "*Thank you.*"

Actually, the hulks in Apartment 12 weren't the only ten-ants harboring an illegal pet. We had an eastern box turtle named Methuselah whom Steph had purchased when she first moved to Iowa, claiming she needed another boyfriend in case it didn't work out with me. We refused to give him away when we moved to OK Apartments after our wedding—we'd miss his pulsating throat, his affectionate hiss, his ancient soul. We adored him. Plus his behavior wasn't likely to betray us to the authorities. Inside the apartment, he'd disappear for days and then, like a good fugitive, sneak out from beneath the couch or refrigerator to demand we hand-feed him smoked turkey, meal worms, and grapes.

Methuselah might have been my role model during my early weeks as maintenance man, as I tried to hide from the other tenants. I lived in fear of the next knock on the door, the next invitation to fail to fix something, the next chance to provoke the wrath of the community. Sometimes, when the phone rang in the early morning, I'd pull the covers over my head and stay there for hours.

It may have been under those covers that I began to recall the happier times I'd spent at Deluca Dwellings, a dumpy foursquare where I'd rented a room starting in my junior year and on into graduate school. It was owned and operated by Clarence C. Deluca, a bald, elderly man who always dressed in the same olive coveralls, zipped too tight at the crotch. During my initial week as a resident of Deluca Dwellings, I received the first of many newsletters Clarence would deliver to me and the other twelve people living in the house. "To the New Lessee," it began, "I say: Welcome to your New Home-Away-From-Home."

> If you are a fan of Astrology, you may take pleasure in the fact that I am a typical Arien. Also, it will not be difficult for you to believe that I will be energetic, enthusiastic and steadfast in my pursuit to be your ideal landlord: not easily discouraged by temporary setbacks; enjoy the challenges of over coming obstacles; like things to be done quickly; whole approach to life is youthful and optimistic; generally gets along with all kinds of people.

YOU, and each of you, are a select person in the strictest meaning of the word. The Landlord is very proud of you and have literally set you upon a pedestal! Therefore, the landlord expects you to be exemplary as tenant in compliance with Agreements including a Clean Dwelling AND the maintenance of your Good Reputation. Enjoy Your Home-Away-From-Home To The Maximum; However, In This Pursuit, Remember That Your Liberty Extends To The Point Of Non-Infringement Upon The Rights Of Others.

QUOTES OF THE MONTH:

Douglas Jerrold: The character that needs law to mend it, is hardly worth the tinkering.

Samuel Smiles: To be worth anything, character must be capable of standing firm upon its feet in the world of daily work, temptation, and trial; and able to bear the wear and tear of actual life. Cloistered virtues do not count for much.

Clarence C. Deluca: Be mindful of other people; and the purity of ones character will manifest itself generously, if one is truly well-meaning.

At first, I found Mr. Deluca's high-minded enthusiasm to be infectious. I was in the process of switching from premedicine to a Religion major, and was in a high-minded mood myself. In addition, the other occupants of the house were the kind of people who, like me, had moved there out of a hard-earned desire for privacy—mostly humanities majors, foreign students, and ex-cons. They made very few social demands, so there was plenty of time to maintain my dwelling and my good reputation. This was publicly acknowledged in the *Deluca Dwellings Newsletter,* Volume 8, Number 4, September 1, 1986:

> UP-AND-COMING STAR: John Price (3-2)—He has demonstrated himself Worthy of his High Character Recommendations and the Trust and Pride of your Landlord by applying a brand new coat of paint to his room and by producing a sparkling Bathroom during his first few months as a resident. Keep Up The Good Work!

> QUOTE OF THE MONTH:
> *Colton:* No man can purchase his virtue too dear, for it is the only thing whose value must ever increase with the price it has cost us. Our integrity is never worth so much as when we have parted with our all to keep it.

Then I got a pet mouse. I can't recall why I purchased him—pets were strictly forbidden at Deluca's. Perhaps it was because my girlfriend had just dumped me or because the consequences of giving up a medical career (again, the girlfriend) had begun to finally hit home. Or perhaps it was the way he appeared at the pet store, the only black mouse crowded in with dozens of whites and browns, all waiting to serve as lunch for someone's boa constrictor.

Whatever the reasons, I brought him home and named him Ernest T. Bass after the mischievous hillbilly on *The Andy Griffith Show.* During the first week, Ernest repeatedly escaped from his cage and, like his TV namesake, thwarted all efforts to contain him. I finally bought him one of those plastic free-rolling hamster spheres, but then, one evening, he rolled out my door and bounced down two flights of stairs. I caught up in time to see him roll into Kurt's room. I stood in the doorway, panicked that this stranger would report my pet to Clarence. Kurt picked the sphere off the floor and grinned at Ernest, who stared back, apparently unfazed by the strange face or the two flights of stairs. During the ensuing conversation, I learned that Kurt was a graduate student in the creative writing program. He was the first serious writer I'd ever met, and the close friendship that developed was one of the reasons I'd become a writer myself. All because of a wayward mouse.

Ernest soon became the house mascot, roaming the halls in his sphere, entering other rooms, and introducing me to more people than I would ever have approached on my own. As a vibrant, sometimes rowdy social life blossomed at Deluca Dwellings, we had less time for maintaining the bathroom on our floor, and its condition rapidly declined. We weren't the only ones who noticed. Despite Clarence's "Arien" optimism, his newsletters became increasingly despondent, culminating in Volume 8, Number 9, April 2, 1987:

EXPOSE!

Landlord Denounces And Labels Four Residents As
Bad Tenants: Namely:
JANE PILLHOUSE JOHN PRICE TRAVIS KING
AND LING-YEOK CHONG
By definition, bad means: failing to reach an acceptable standard. FACT: The Bad Tenants named above failed to

meet the Clean Bathroom standard during the "Mandatory Clean Bathroom Days" of March 15th and 29th, 1987.

Disclaimer: The intent of the Expose is not to slander the persons named (for by definition, the truth and slander are incongruent), but to use a reasonable means, namely: Embarrassment (a state of self-conscious distress), within the limited confines of this Dwelling Family, in an attempt to correct a Health Hazard.

The Landlord hopes that this "public" revelation has done its intended job well; that a wise attitude of course of action subsequently will reflect intelligence commensurate with their chronological age and apparent educational status; that the 4-Bad Tenants are not incorrigible and will recall and heed the good home training taught by their parents; that the Characteristic which carries the label "BAD" shall be discarded for the label "GOOD."

Two adages are worth repeating here: "Character Will Out" AND "Time Will Tell."

The Landlord hereby makes apology to all except the 4-Bad Tenants for terminating the letter at this point. The frustration and depression which has resulted in the writing of this report consumed all the energy and enthusiasm which is usually devoted to an "up-beat" communication . . .

QUOTE OF THE MONTH:

Aeschines: He who acts wickedly in private life, can never be expected to show himself noble in public conduct; he that is base at home will not acquit himself with honor abroad; for it is not the man, but only the place that is changed.

In addition to being distributed to every resident of the house, the letter was sent to parents and to those who'd written recommendations, among them our bosses, professors, and spiritual mentors.

"He sent this to Reverend Hearn, for godsakes!" my mother shouted into the phone. "He makes it sound like you all crap in the bathtub—*What's going on over there?*"

In response to this humiliation, my floormates and I cranked our favorite Smiths song—"Sweet and Tender Hooligan"—and spent the afternoon scrubbing porcelain, pausing only to drink more beer or pay homage to Ernest, who directed us from his cage on the back of the toilet. In a generous spirit, we even cleaned the bathrooms on the other floors, helping Kurt overcome his orange-streaked, mildewy shower stall. A month later, to my mother's relief, we were publicly exonerated in the *Deluca Dwellings Newsletter:*

> YES, a single happening! And that's all it takes sometimes to make or break one for life: remember Wallace?, Agnue?, Nixon? And Hart? This single accomplishment (Bathroom Cleaning) may be construed "virtuous" (demonstrating "a commendable quality" and "conformity to a standard of what is right and good"). For anyone who may be struggling and are now vindicated, your Landlord suggests that you "exercise" your integrity (however small and weak). Consequently, if you are truly one of goodwill (predisposed to conform to sanctioned codes or accepted notions of right and wrong,) your Character shall "grow" and become "strong."

My floormates and I celebrated by filling the bathtub with ice, purchasing a pony keg, and throwing a house party. All night, amidst the revelry and dancing legs, the guest of honor rolled in his plastic sphere.

Ernest lived another year or so before dying peacefully in his sleep. When I told my neighbors, there was general sadness—we had lost one of our own. At a sunset funeral in the front yard, Kurt read a poem while others tossed violets and small bundles of seed into the grave. I remained close to several of them, including Kurt, who took off for Los Angeles to become a screenplay writer. A few years later, he was murdered in an attempt to steal his car. The last time I saw him, during one of his brief visits from California, we sat in our favorite bar reminiscing about Deluca Dwellings and about Ernest. We lifted our glasses to the memory of a lost friend.

⚬⟋⟋⚬

Recollections of Kurt and Ernest and the fellowship enjoyed at Deluca Dwellings amplified my misery at OK Apartments. I tried to convince myself that our social isolation was due to the layout of the buildings: Each unit looked out on the dirty concrete of the parking lot. This place lacked the character and intimacy of Mr. Deluca's old house. A more likely reason, which I'm sure Steph suspected, was my disastrous skills as a handyman. After several more half days without water, people became openly hostile toward me: sour looks, prank calls, screaming. One person scooped the feces out of his unflushable toilet and dumped them on our doorstep.

The only friend I really had there was Ted. He was always pleasant, even when I called him after midnight to help with a plumbing emergency, but his wife, Janet, was a hard knot of repressed anger, lashing out at tenants (and me) for the smallest infractions. Unlike the other tenant complaints, Janet's criticism barely registered: I felt too sorry for her, for both of them. Ted once told me that he and Janet had enjoyed a passionate affair when they were our age and, following a hasty wedding, were full of big plans: She would be a photojournalist and he a structural engineer for sports coliseums. Now they were in their forties, had a teenage daughter, and lived in a small apartment surrounded by college students, most of whom drove better cars than they did. Whenever I visited their place, the claustrophobia was as thick as the smell of shaving cream and hamburger grease that seemed to be always hovering in the air. Three bicycles hung from the ceiling above their couch, next to plywood wall shelves overflowing with family photos, knickknacks, and golf videos. To their credit, Ted and Janet had carved out a pink refuge in the second bedroom for their daughter, Eveline. Their bedroom was a blizzard of discarded clothes that often hung, dripping, from the unused Stairmaster doubling as a nightstand and plant holder.

This was a version of the future Steph and I didn't need to see. We were only just discovering that being married involves the art of having simultaneous emotional breakdowns in the same room. Steph was finding the experience of student teaching to be something akin to exorcism, while I was beginning to question seriously my decision to pursue a doctoral degree in English. Things culminated, for me, during comprehensive exams—a brutal experience after which I purchased a bottle of gin, collapsed in front of the TV, and watched, over and over again, the *Hallmark Hall of Fame*'s presentation of *O Pioneers!*

Late at night, Steph and I often talked about relinquishing the traditional life and moving to a small town in Idaho or Oregon, where she'd open a bead shop and I'd write best-selling novels. We'd wake up groggy with hope, until one of us bumped into Ted or Janet and was reminded of what happens when risky dreams go bad. Lying on our couch, we could almost see the bicycles swinging, like pendulums, above our necks.

In December, Jerry called to announce they'd experienced the biggest mid-year flight of tenants in memory, and asked if I knew why. I expressed surprise, but suspected it might have something to do with the combination of my poor plumbing skills and Janet's poor attitude. A week later, Jerry called to tell me that they were flooded with new applications. Once again, he asked if I knew why. I didn't, but eventually discovered that the tenants in 12—Ditka's boys—had spread word around our university town that OK Apartments was pet-friendly. I was soon introduced to Paula the parakeet and Fernando the ferret and Satan the albino boa constrictor, as well as a number of other new tenants who had rushed to our complex as if it were the ark.

At first, the dramatic increase in illegal pets made me even more anxious, but those feelings soon became lost in the newly elevated spirit at OK. Suddenly, it was a much friendlier place—people dropped by to say hello or to invite us to dinner or keg parties. Some even volunteered to help with small fix-it jobs. Over the next few months many of us became friends. And as our affection grew for each other, so did our affection for each other's pets. The women in 18 made a weekly habit of dropping off organic greens from the co-op for Methuselah, while I became especially attached to a pair of mice—AC and DC—owned by the heavy-metal guys in 21, even giving them Ernest's old traveling sphere. All this without any noticeable change in my skills as a handyman. What had changed was the community itself—now largely composed of people willing to go without water for a few hours every week if it meant they wouldn't have to go without the animals they loved.

For a while, we were able to keep our little ecosystem secret. Janet, unlike me, had to give twenty-four-hour notice before entering an apartment, so tenants had plenty of time to hide their pets with neighbors. But then one morning Janet spotted Ditka grooming himself in the window and immediately alerted Kenneth, Jerry's usually silent business partner. Kenneth gave the tenants the opportunity to give up their cat, but they refused. He promptly evicted them, minus their damage deposit. I watched in sadness as they loaded up their rusted Escort and drove away, Ditka perched in the rear window. I had to admire them: Instead of giving Ditka to the shelter, they'd given up their own shelter—no easy thing in winter, in the middle of a semester.

A few minutes later, Janet knocked on the door.

"I just talked to Jerry," she said. "He's very upset that Kenneth had to deal with this mess. *Very* upset. He said you had strict instructions to report any animal activity to him. And by the way, how exactly did you miss seeing that cat? You've been over there a thousand times fixing your mistakes."

I gave her some lame excuse, but she was clearly suspicious.

"You'd better be careful," she warned, "or you'll lose your job."

This time, Janet's threat hit the mark. From under the covers, I considered the fact that if I lost this job, we wouldn't be able to pay the rent. Like Ditka's owners, we'd be cast out into the dismal winter, where, the price of virtue aside, finding an affordable place would be nearly impossible. There's no question whom our families would blame; I could already hear Steph's father: *First year of marriage and he has them living in the streets!*

Later that week, I got a call from the women in 19, who said their toilet had been running all night. I grudgingly gathered my tools and, after knocking repeatedly on their door, let myself in. Inside the bathroom, I spotted Chowder, their rabbit. Chowder was brown and huge—the biggest rabbit I'd ever seen—and his flabby bulk was stretched out between the base of the toilet and the wall. "Hi, guy," I said in an overly friendly tone that, in retrospect, I probably hadn't earned. When I reached down near his belly for the water shutoff valve, Chowder let out a horrifying screech and attacked my forearm with his sharp claws and teeth. I fell backward onto the floor, kicking at my surprisingly animated assailant until, still screeching, he retreated to the bedroom.

While washing my wounds in the sink, I resolved to tell Jerry about Chowder. There were several good reasons. First, the fat freak had attacked me. Second, his owners were the kind of women—tall, beautiful, and aloof—who tapped into several residual teenage resentments. Third, and most important, by betraying this bad animal I might not only save my job, but I might also protect the other, good animals in the complex. Jerry's trust would be restored, so he wouldn't go snooping around the apartments. The individual would be sacrificed, but, as Aldo Leopold directed, the general health of the biotic community would be maintained.

When I announced my plan to Steph, I became the victim of another unexpected attack. She questioned, loudly, how I could ever think of doing such a thing. She recalled some of the animals I'd cared about in my life, including Ernest. "Imagine what Mr. Deluca would've done to that mouse!" she said. "It's an evil plan, John. Even if you do get caught, we'll find another place. We'll live."

"Yeah, but where?" I replied, and stormed out of the apartment.

In the dim cave of the laundry room, I paced a row of yawning dryers and tried to convince myself that Steph had no right to say those things to me. Conjuring up old Clarence had been a particularly low blow—I did know what he would've done had he caught Ernest. I recalled a conversation we'd had during my final week at Deluca Dwellings. Clarence sat in my red corduroy recliner, having just finished the final bathroom inspection, scolding me for another poor score (things had gone downhill after Ernest passed away). He wondered aloud what my family would think of my behavior, which prompted me to wonder what Mr. Deluca's family thought of his. Actually, I didn't know if he had any living family. I'd guessed from a few short visits to his house—a small, cluttered ranch near a strip mall—that he lived alone. No pictures stuck to the refrigerator, no birthdays scribbled on the wall calendar, no dog toys or cat litter on the floor. After all those years, the man was still a blank to me.

"You're a student of the Bible, aren't you, John?" he asked, though he'd once congratulated me for being named the Religion

Department's "Outstanding Student of Judaica." He'd even introduced me—a Congregationalist—to a prospective Jewish tenant
as having won the award for "Top Jew at the University of Iowa."
This had been one sign among many that it was time to leave.

"Yes, I'm a student of the Bible."

"Well, you'd never know it. I've been rereading the book of
Amos, which I strongly suggest you review. In that book, God
destroys all the cities that displease Him. Contrary to several so-
called theological opinions, I have no disagreement with God's
harsh treatment. He warned his people, he was merciful, but
they continued to break his laws. It's as if you made some human
or animal figures out of putty, but they didn't meet your stan-
dards. What do you do with them? Well, you *smash* them and
start over!" He drove his fist into his palm, probably to illustrate
what he was about to do to my damage deposit. But years later,
pacing the laundry room at OK Apartments, what I pictured was
the jellied body of Ernest running between his fingers.

I was still unsure what to do—I was no longer a boy living
on my own. I stared into one of the chicken wire storage units
at a tattered corduroy recliner. It was similar to the one Clarence
had sat in to deliver that final sermon. Years before, my friend
Kurt had sat in the same recliner on the eve of departing for LA.
Earlier that day, I'd helped Kurt move his furniture into the
basement of his family's home in Dubuque. I'd asked him about
the people pictured on the living-room wall, his parents, his
brother, about whom he told several affectionate stories. Upon
returning to Deluca's, Kurt had sat in my recliner and confessed
he'd been thinking of calling the whole move off. He said that
in all the excitement of leaving Iowa, he hadn't anticipated feel-

ing so attached to friends and family. He got quiet for a while, stood up, embraced me, and left.

That's when I knew: I wouldn't betray Chowder and his owners. I wouldn't betray any of them. They had a right, those people and those animals, to live together and be happy. They had a right, quite simply, to live.

The rest of the semester went surprisingly well; no one was caught harboring illegal animals. On the personal front, Steph landed a teaching job near the small town of Belle Plaine, about an hour away, and I was awarded a small dissertation scholarship. We'd be moving to the countryside, just the way we'd dreamed.

Things weren't going as well for Ted and Janet. On our last day they were hosting a high school graduation party for their daughter, and it was raining heavily, as it would most of that summer. Earlier in the week, I'd treated Ted to lunch to thank him for all his help. He surprised me by revealing that he and Janet were going to file for divorce as soon as Eveline left for college. They'd kept it together for her sake, he said, but there was no longer love there, not even much friendship. He invited us to attend Eveline's party, but now, watching their silent guests eat sloppy joes on the wet balcony above the Dumpsters, we decided to keep packing.

While Steph was off gathering boxes, someone knocked on the door. It was Jerry, holding a paper plate with a soggy, half-eaten slice of cake on it. He said he'd decided to drop by to return our damage deposit and to ask a favor. It was time to renew leases, he said, and though Janet was supposed to make the final inspections of the apartments, she was busy with the party. He wondered if I would mind doing a quick run-through on my own. I'd completely forgotten about the final inspection, which might've spelled disaster for us all. This fortunate visit from Jerry, along with the fact that I'd convinced him to hire a friend of mine—another animal lover—to be the next maintenance man, suggested the purity of my character was, as Mr. Deluca had promised, manifesting itself generously.

"I'm happy to do it."

"Thanks," he said, stepping inside. "If you don't mind, I'll just park myself here until you get back. I have some deposit checks to write."

Although school was out, there were quite a few people in the complex, and this gave me a chance to say good-bye to them and their pets. I even said good-bye to Chowder, with whom I'd long been reconciled. At last count, there were five cats, four hamsters, three parakeets, two rabbits, two ferrets, two mice, a green water dragon, a snake, and numerous fish (which weren't technically illegal, though I took moral credit for them anyway). Ascending the stairs to our apartment, I carried the satisfaction that this little community, this dwelling family, had become more diverse, more integral, than when we'd arrived—a collective strength of character that, to recall another favorite quote of Mr. Deluca's, should require no law to mend.

When I stepped through the doorway, Jerry was sitting on our couch reading the paper.

"How'd it go?" he asked, without looking up.

"Fine," I replied, then saw something move in the background. Methuselah, probably disturbed by our packing, had decided to emerge from his hiding place and was now in the middle of the floor. Jerry put the paper down, stretched, and stood up.

"Thanks again for all your help," he said, walking past me through the doorway. He stopped and turned. "Oh, yeah. Did you find any animals?"

"No," I said. Methuselah's claws scraped loudly against the kitchen linoleum. Jerry's eyes shifted over my shoulder, into the apartment. At that moment, despite my earlier conviction, despite everything, I was ready to confess, ready to turn us all over to his mercy. Before I could speak, Jerry handed me the check for our damage deposit. The amount in full.

"Well," he said, smiling, "that's a relief."

Man Killed by Pheasant

So I'm driving east on Highway 30, from our new home in Belle Plaine to Cedar Rapids, Iowa. It's a four-lane, and because I'm an eldest child, I'm driving the speed limit, around fifty-five, sixty miles per hour. I'm listening to Jimi Hendrix cry "Mary"—imagining, as usual, that I am Jimi Hendrix—when in the far distance I see some brown blobs hovering across the highway: one, then two. By the way they move, low and slow, I suspect they're young pheasants. As I near the place of their crossing I look over the empty passenger seat and into the grassy ditch to see if I can spot the whole clan. Suddenly, there is a peripheral darkness, the fast shadow of an eclipse, and something explodes against the side of my head in a fury of flapping and scratching and squawking. In an act of extraordinary timing, one of the straggling pheasants has flown in my driver's side window. And being the steel-jawed action hero I am, I scream, scream like a rabbit, and strike at it frantically with my left arm, the car swerving, wings snapping, Hendrix wailing, feathers beating at my face until, at last, I knock the thing back out the window and onto the road. I regain control of the car, if not myself, and pull over, undone.

That's the time I should have been killed by a pheasant. For reasons peculiar to that summer, I recall it often. It occurred, for one, while I was on my way to teach a technical writing course at a nearby community college, a summer job to help me through grad school. This "distance learning experience" took place exclusively by radio wave, with me in an empty room on campus and my fifteen students scattered at sites within a hundred-mile radius. The technology was such that my students could see me, but I couldn't see them. To converse we had to push buttons at the base of our microphones, so that each class felt like an episode of *Larry King Live: Judy, from Monticello, hello, you're on the air.* "The future of higher education" my supervisor called it. And I never did get the hang of the camera. I'd turn it on at the beginning of class and there, on the big-screen monitor, would be a super-close-up of my lips. I'd spend the next few minutes jostling the joystick, zooming in and out like one of those early music videos until I found the suitable frame. Sometimes my students would laugh at this, and I'd hear them laughing, but only if they pushed their buttons. If there was an electrical storm nearby, I wouldn't hear them at all.

On the way to such a displaced, bodiless job, a near-death experience had some additional currency. As did the larger natural disaster unfolding around me. It was the summer of the great Iowa floods, 1993, and the reason I was on Highway 30 to begin with was that my usual route to campus had been washed out by the swollen Iowa River. This was a serious situation: People had been killed and Des Moines had been without water for over a week. "Nature Gone Mad!" was how the national media described it.

Although aware of the widespread suffering, I was privileged to watch the whole thing unfold more gently from the roadways of my rural commutes. And what I saw was a wilderness of birds. Bean fields suddenly became sheer, inaccessible places where herons stood piercing frogs in the shallows, where pelicans flew in great cyclonic towers, where bald eagles swung low to pick off stranded fish. Perched on soggy, neglected fence posts were birds I hadn't seen since early childhood, bobolinks and bluebirds and tanagers. Their color and song drew my eye closer to the earth, to the ragged ditches full of forgotten wildflowers and grasses—primrose and horsemint, big blue and switch—safe, at least for a while, from the mower's blade. The domesticated landscape of my home had gone wild and I was mesmerized by it.

Toward the end of the summer flooding, when the dramatic presence of wild birds dwindled, I thought a lot about Noah, about those end days on the Ark between the release of the raven and the return of the dove, between knowledge of a decimated landscape and faith in one that, through decimation, had become reborn. When it was all over, I thought I understood Noah's first impulse, once on dry land, to get drunk and forget. I'd lived my entire life in Iowa, the most ecologically altered state in the union, with less than one-tenth of 1 percent of its native habitats remaining. "Tragic" is what the ecologist Wes Jackson has called the plowing up of this prairie region, "one of the two or three worst atrocities committed by Americans." Not that I'd ever cared—it's hard to care about a wild place you've never seen or known. Yet in those short, flooded months of 1993, I witnessed a blurry reflection of what the land had once been: a rich ecology of wetlands and savannahs and prairies, alive with movement and migration. Alive with power. Under its influence, I felt closer to my home landscape than ever before. So when that power slipped from view, I was surprised to find myself longing to chase after it. Having spent most of my life wanting to leave the Midwest, where might I find the reasons to stay, to commit?

Death by pheasant didn't immediately come to mind. Although, in the wake of the floods, death was part of what I longed for. Or rather the possibility of a certain kind of death, the kind in which you become lost in a vast landscape and die, as Edward Abbey has described it, "alone, on rock under sun at the brink of the unknown, like a wolf, like a great bird." This had nearly been my fate on that cliff in Idaho, during our honeymoon, and in my mind it helped define that wilderness as a place worthy of respect, a place of consequence and a kind of fearful freedom. My German friend, Elmar, calls this freedom *vogelfrei*, which loosely translates into "free as a bird." Far from the positive spin we've put on this phrase, *vogelfrei* refers to the state of being cast out from the tribe, so free you'll die in the open, unburied, to be picked apart by birds. It's a state of fear and vulnerability and movement, one that might, especially here in the agricultural Midwest—a place seemingly without fang or claw or talon—make us more attentive to the natural world, more humbled by its power to transform us.

At first flush, my collision with the pheasant didn't seem to hold that kind of possibility. But it could have. If, for example, this had happened to me as a child or adolescent or as a member of a New Age men's group, I might have made something more

of it. When I was a boy, some of my favorite comic book characters were mutations of man and animal—Mole Man, of
course, and Spiderman and Captain America's ally, the Falcon.
Imagine the comic book story that could have developed this
time: A mild-mannered English professor is struck in the head
by a wayward pheasant, his blood mingling with the bird's
while, coincidentally, a cosmic tsunami from a distant stellar ex-
plosion soaks the whole scene in gamma radiation. Emerging
from the smoldering rubble: Pheasant Man. No, *Super* Pheasant
Man! As Super Pheasant Man, our mild-mannered professor
finds he has acquired the bird's more powerful features—its
pride and daring, its resilience, its colorful head feathers—learning to use them for the good of humanity while at the same
time fighting the darker side of his condition, namely, a propen-
sity for polygamy and loose stools.

But I was not a boy when I met that unlucky pheasant on
Highway 30, which is too bad, because for a long time afterward I found nothing particularly uplifting about the experience. Instead, I saw my life, and death, made a joke. Imagine
the regional headlines: *Iowa Man Killed by Pheasant; Mother
Files for Hunting License.* Imagine the funeral, where, in the
middle of "I'll Fly Away," one of my more successful cousins
whispers to his wife, *You know, it wasn't even a cock pheasant that
killed him. It was just a little baby pheasant.* Imagine the members of that hypothetical men's group, who, in their wailful
mourning of my death, botch up the spirit animal ritual and
condemn my soul to be borne not on the wings of an eagle or a
falcon, but on those of a pheasant, stubby and insufficient,
struggling to get us both off the ground, never getting more

than maybe fifteen feet toward heaven before dropping back down to earth with a thud and a cluck.

No, thank you. I do not wish to become one with the pheasant, in this life or in the next. Yet seen through the history of the land, this bird and I have been colliding for centuries. Having evolved together on the grasslands of distant continents, we were both brought to this country by the accidents of nature and technology and desire. As Americans, the pheasant and I have come to share certain important historical figures, like Benjamin Franklin, whose son-in-law was one of the first to attempt to introduce the ring-necked pheasant, a native of China, to this country—an unsuccessful release in New Jersey. Its introduction to Iowa over a century later was by accident, taking place during a 1901 windstorm near Cedar Falls that blew down confinement fences and released two thousand of the birds into the prairie night. They've remained here ever since, sharing with my people an affinity for the Northern Plains to which we've both become anchored by the peculiarities of the soil. This soil, loess and glacial till, is migrant and invasive, like us, having been carried here from ancient Canada by wind and by ice. Its rich, organic loam, black as oil, brought my farmer ancestors to the region and has, at the same time, held close the range of the ring-necked pheasant, lacing the bird's grit with calcium carbonate. Because the ring-neck requires an abundance of this mineral, it doesn't stray far, not even a few hundred miles south into the gray prairies of, say, lower Illinois.

So the pheasant and I have remained settlers in this region, watching as others of our kind move on. As such, we have come to share some of the same enemies, like the fencerow-to-

fenccrow, get-big-or-get-out agricultural policies of the 1970s
and '80s. These policies, enacting yet another vision of migration, dramatically expanded agricultural exports and, at the
same time, led the region to the farm crisis of the 1980s, to the
flight and impoverishment and death of thousands of industrial
and farm families. For the pheasant as well, despite set-aside
programs, this fencerow-to-fencerow world has held its own
kind of impoverishment, a destruction of habitat so thorough
that two hundred pheasants have been known to crowd a shel-
terbelt only a hundred yards long. In such a bare-naked world a
good blizzard, like the one in 1975—while I was honking truck
horns with my grandfather—has the power to wipe out 80 percent of a local pheasant population in a single evening.

Yet, in sharing enemies, we have also been, together, the
common enemy. To the prairie chicken, for instance—one of
the many native citizens that had the unfortunate luck to pre-
cede us here in the "heartland." For almost a century European
settlers hunted and plowed down prairie chicken populations in
Iowa. But the ring-necked pheasant has also played a role, destroying the prairie chicken's eggs, occupying its nests, and in-
terrupting, seemingly out of spite, its dancing-ground rituals.
Some argue that restoring prairie chicken populations will have
to coincide with significant reductions in pheasant populations.
Reducing pheasant numbers around here, however, is about as
easy and popular as reducing our own. The difficulties are partly
economic: In Iowa, we hunt and eat this bird to the tune of
about a million and a half a year. It's one of our biggest tourist
attractions. But I wonder, too, if we don't see in this bird, at
some unconscious level, a dark reflection of our own troubling

history in the American grasslands, our role as ecological party crashers, as culture wreckers. Our role, ultimately, as killers and thieves. To question the pheasant's claim on the land is, in some way, to question our own.

It's unfair, of course, and dangerous to project our sins onto another species. When tossing around ethical responsibility, the difference between us, between instinct and intent, is significant. But the pheasants needn't worry about taking the blame. Hardly anyone around here gives them a second thought. That indifference was part of my problem when I finally began searching, while living in Belle Plaine, for reasons to care about my home landscape. In relation to that bird, as to most of the familiar, transplanted wildlife around me, I felt nothing. The pheasant was common, and the last thing I wanted to feel as a Midwesterner was common. Since early adolescence I'd been fleeing a sense of inadequacy shared by many in this region, a sense of self marked—as Minnesotan Patricia Hampl has said— by "an indelible brand of innocence, which is to be marked by an absence, a vacancy. By nothing at all." For Midwesterners like me, the complex, the worthy seemed always to be found elsewhere. Not here in this ordinary place, this ordinary life.

Not surprisingly, in the years immediately following the flood, I didn't seek that new relationship to the Midwest in the familiar land immediately around me, but by traveling to distant and, in my imagination, more exotic landscapes such as the Black Hills and Badlands in western South Dakota. What I discovered in those places did indeed transform me. Near Wind Cave, I saw for the first time elk bugling and mating at home on their native prairies. While sitting in a fly-plagued prairie dog town, I saw for the first time a bison bull wallowing in the brown dust. On the grasslands near Bear Butte, where Crazy Horse once sought vision, I saw for the first time a falcon stoop to kill a duck, the native cycles of predator and prey, of wild death, still lingering. Even *vogelfrei*, that fearful freedom—I felt it for the first time in this region while walking lost in the deep earth of the Badlands. My journey through these places toward commitment has been awkward, fragmented, and at times pathetic, even comic. Yet the significance of those experiences cannot be underestimated, how they have worked to cure a lifetime of ignorance and indifference. How, to use spiritual terms, they have filled what once was empty.

But if the spiritual journey to a place begins, as some claim, with mortal fear, then it was not the bison or the falcon or the Badlands that first drew me closer to the region in which I'd been raised. It was the pheasant, that particular baby pheasant—there on a highway in eastern Iowa—which almost, as my sister Allyson would say, rocked my world. In a sense, that's exactly what it did. It made me wake up, become more observant of what's lurking in the margins. What's lurking there, despite the rumors, is the possibility of surprise, of accident, of death. And if it's possible in this overdetermined landscape for a pheasant to kill a man, then why not also the possibility of restoration, renewal, and, at last, hope?

That's a romantic stretch, I know, and at the time of the incident itself I didn't feel particularly worshipful of its surprise. As I sat in the car, wiping my face, I just felt lucky—*Thank God it wasn't a two-lane!*—and then ridiculous. The whole thing was so absurd it might've been a dream. I carefully leaned my head out the window to see if the pheasant was still on the road. It wasn't. I thought about going back to see if it was injured, but decided against it—after all, it was only a pheasant. Besides, I was late for work, where in a few minutes I would be taking my own precarious flight through the airwaves, across the flooded land, to students I would never see, never truly know.

I started the car and eased back onto the highway. As I approached cruising speed I saw something move out of the corner of my eye. I jerked, swerving the car a little. A feather. An ordinary brown feather. Then another and another—there must have been a dozen—floating in the breeze of the open window. They tickled and annoyed me. Yet for reasons I still can't explain, I kept the window open, just a crack, enough to keep the feathers dancing about the cabin. And that's how I, the man almost killed by a pheasant, drove the rest of those miles, touched by its feathers in flight, touched by an intimacy as rare and welcome, in my tragic country, as laughter in a storm.

Prairie Asinus

The first time I encountered the "begging burros" of Custer State Park was during a family trip to the Black Hills in the summer of 1975, when Mom was pregnant with my youngest sister, Allyson. We were on our way to Disneyland in California, and our parents had decided to take a northern detour through South Dakota, retracing the route they'd followed during their honeymoon in the early sixties. Interstate 90 had its attractions back then—the life-sized dinosaur statues in Sioux Falls, the Corn Palace in Mitchell—but mostly it was long and hot, and to pass the hours my sisters and I formed a band: Iowa Freedom. The name was inspired by Elton John's "Philadelphia Freedom," one of our father's favorite songs, though that didn't win us any favors. Whenever the concerts got too rowdy or the musicians suffered the inevitable artistic differences, Dad would click off the radio and return his elbow to its place of contentment on the edge of the open window. With nothing better to do, my sisters and I would shift our attention to the outside world, which, at some point past the Missouri River, completely changed. The corn retreated as if it were a fog, the black earth became cream, and the heavy wet air of home became dry and light, like a big clean breath, held, then let go.

We spent our first evening in the Black Hills watching Jesus get crucified in the "World Famous" Spearfish Passion Play. The next day was even more loaded: Mount Rushmore, Crazy Horse Monument, Sylvan Lake, Bear Country U.S.A., and finally Custer State Park. By the time we pulled into the parking lot of the State Game Lodge, the sun was approaching the tops of the pine-covered hills, but Dad thought there was time enough to see the bison. He flagged down a park official, who generously agreed to give us a tour of the herd in his open-air jeep, safari style. Soon we were among them, the bison cows and calves meandering out of the shaded grassland and onto the road, the bulls off by themselves, scratching their massive woolly heads against tree stumps. When they got too close, Susan would whimper and tuck her head against Mom; they were the biggest, wildest, most amazing animals I'd ever seen. Later during that trip, Carrie Anne nearly choked to death on a buffalo burger and I could understand why. Bison were too big for Custer State Park—too big for my imagination, it seemed—and certainly too big to be placed on a hamburger bun and eaten by my little sister.

The burros were something else altogether. A dozen or so were waiting for us on the road back to the lodge, an odd conglomeration of size and color, some approaching the stature of horses, though most were stunted and swaybacked, bellies hanging just above their knobby knees. What they were doing in that wild place, so close to the bison, was beyond me, but they demonstrated no such ambivalence over their role in the local ecosystem. The largest parked himself directly in the path of the jeep, and the rest quickly surrounded us, cutting off all routes of escape—a strategic ambush that defied their dim-witted reputation. Before our driver could stop her, Carrie Anne offered up a corn chip, and the frenzied attack that followed still haunts my nightmares: Their bristled snouts swarmed against us, snorting and braying, baring their mossy teeth and putting their wet lips on our arms, legs, and faces. We were all screaming. Dad finally barked at the driver to "hit it" and he was eventually able to maneuver the jeep through a small opening in the wall of burr- and fly-infested hide, but not before we lost the entire bag of corn chips, several nibble-sized pieces of clothing and shoelace, and half of Mom's wiglet. Back at the lodge, after vigorous bathing, we ate our dinner in silence under the constant, but courteous, gaze of the mounted heads of bison and other native wildlife.

It was twenty years before I met up with the burros again, in the fall of 1995. I was not on my way to visit Disneyland, but to visit native prairie, which, I had learned, could be another kind of Fantasyland. The year before, I'd spent my first night camping in the open grasslands, pitching my tent in nearby Buffalo Gap National Grasslands, during a cold June drizzle. I spent most of the night peering out of the mosquito netting, hoping that the place would turn out to be like the wild prairies I'd read about in accounts of early explorers. "The sea, the woods, the mountains, all suffer in comparison with the prairie," proclaimed Albert Pike in the 1830s. "Its sublimity arises from its unbounded extent, its barren monotony and desolation, its still, unmoved, calm, stern, almost self-confident grandeur, its strange power of deception, its want of echo, and, in fine, its power of throwing a man back upon himself." That's what I craved—sublimity, grandeur, power—the indigenous character of the land I'd first glimpsed during the Iowa floods.

What I experienced instead, at least at first, was deception. After the drizzle cleared, I spied tiny lights moving in the far distance which I imagined—wished—into the moon-illumined eyes of bison or elk, or maybe the spectral gaze of prehistoric creatures whose bones still inhabited the deep earth of that country. They turned out to be the headlights of cars and semis on Interstate 90. And the mysterious snuffling and stomping near my tent before dawn? A heifer grazing on invasive yellow clover. There were other embarrassing, even dangerous, missteps during that first trip, such as pitching my tent in a buffalo wallow and hiking off into the Badlands without an adequate supply of water or a compass. Igniting my kerosene stove in the middle of all that dry grass, as I did several times, had been the intellectual equivalent of Yosemite Sam striking a match in a shack of dynamite. I should've been incarcerated or killed—*vogelfrei,* at last.

Nevertheless, that initial, ill-prepared excursion into the grasslands indelibly changed my relationship to the land. For the first time I had chosen to make myself vulnerable to place, and had emerged more respectful of and more committed to what was left of wildness in my home region. More humble, as well. But old humiliations die hard and, as with adolescent classmates, tend to inspire elaborate reunions where all (in theory) will be redeemed. Those were certainly my feelings when I'd attended my tenth high school reunion in Fort Dodge the previous summer, coming together with people painfully familiar with my Mole Man years, trying at least partially to erase that earlier image of myself, only to discover that they had mostly forgotten it. That's how I felt now, as I returned alone to the place where I'd first fallen in love with the wild grasslands, and acted the fool because of it. This time, I planned to camp in the open air of Wind Cave National Park, best known for the massive underground cave regarded by the Lakota as a sacred site of origin, where Buffalo Woman emerged and gave bison to their people. I'd learned that the park included one of the largest, most successful and diverse prairie restorations in the region. This time, camping on that prairie, I would prove (at least to myself) that I knew what I was doing, that I carried within me more than just desire and dream. This time, I would prove that I belonged.

Before going to Wind Cave, I decided for sentimental reasons to return to some of the Black Hills locales I'd visited with my family in 1975, including Custer State Park, which reminded me that places are just as capable as individuals of making fools of themselves. Why would the state of South Dakota suffer anything to be named after a homicidal maniac like George Armstrong Custer? Even as a child, it bothered me. Nelson Greenwood had told me plenty about General Custer, how he'd charged through peaceful Indian villages at sunrise and killed every man, woman, and child he could get his sights on. Nelson's story was, as usual, validated by my secondary sources at the time. While brushing up for the trip to the Magic Kingdom I'd encountered an illustrated story, entitled "Tonka," in one of our Disney anthologies. In one illustration, General Custer was shown interrogating a young Sioux warrior, shaking the boy by the scruff and explaining how important it is "that these red savages learn who is running the country! They must learn quickly—or be wiped out!" In another illustration, Custer was himself getting wiped out at Little Bighorn. There wasn't a depiction of the general's particular end, but Nelson informed me that, after the battle, Indian women jabbed sticks into his ears so he would become a better listener. That seemed a little harsh, but even the Disney story hinted he may have been asking for it.

When I entered the park itself, however, all the mistakes of the past seemed to temporarily dissipate. The hills, thick with ponderosa pine, and with shrubs that had turned their autumn crimson and gold, enfolded then released me into the grassy bottomlands. Back among the bison, who were grazing amid the smoke-topped Indian grass and gossamer switch, I became almost giddy, which reminded me of the strange effect the place had had on my parents, decades ago. Whatever cares they'd shouldered back then, about traveling cross-country with three young children or about the new pregnancy, seemed to vanish as they revisited the sites of their early marriage, the origins of our very existence, though we hardly appreciated it. The hand-holding, the giggling, the kisses snuck when they thought my sisters and I weren't looking—all of it disgusted us, further delaying progress toward the true destination: Disneyland. Our parents behaved as if there was no such thing as progress, or linear time, and there were moments when we wondered aloud if they'd keep us there *forever*. Now, as my car moved slowly along the Wildlife Loop, as I inhaled the musk of the bison, the sharp, almost painful drafts of pinesap and grass, I could understand the temptation.

When I saw the begging burros closing in on my car, I felt a brief swell of nostalgia: There they were, just like back then. No linear time, no years. How sweet. Then I stopped, and one of them stuck his entire head in the window and began searching my crumb-littered lap with his tongue. I managed to push him back and roll up the window, but that only encouraged them. A dozen salivating lips pressed at once against the glassy surfaces of the car, mucking up the view and the mood. All sorts of derogatory associations came to mind, such as those guys who ambush you at city intersections to wash your windows, then demand payment. Or coastal seagulls. During a trip to New York, I had taken a boat ride with friends to see Ellis Island, to visit the place where my great-grandmother Tillie, only twenty-eight years old, dreams still intact, had first entered the country. Another sacred site of origin, I suppose. As our boat passed beneath the outstretched arm of Liberty, we unpacked our lunch of pepperoni rolls and were immediately accosted by a raving, crap-spewing cyclone of gulls, as well as the vicious insults of our shipmates. As then, I waved my arms at the offensive creatures, trying to fend them off.

"Begone, Asinus!"

Here was another derogatory association, this time literary—I was still trying to finish my dissertation. Asinus was the comical donkey in James Fenimore Cooper's 1827 novel *The Prairie*, which I'd read during my initial semester of graduate school. It was the first serious novel I'd encountered that made use of the wild grasslands of my home region, though the perspective wasn't particularly accurate or uplifting. At one point, Natty Bumpo, or "Hawkeye," the aging hero of Cooper's Leatherstocking Tales, exclaimed, "I often think the Lord has placed this barren belt of prairie behind the States to warn men to what their folly may yet bring the land!" As if to illustrate that point, Cooper included the characters of Dr. Obed Bat, a "small," pompous naturalist who traveled to the prairies to collect various specimens of native flora and fauna, along with his donkey, *Asinus domesticus Americanus*—Asinus, for short. Both proved to be largely useless to the major characters, even hazardous, though Dr. Bat provided some comic relief and the spastic braying of Asinus did save everyone from a hostile Indian attack and stampeding bison. Despite these accidental heroics, Asinus remained, in the words of one heroine, "a patient, hard-working hack." Even his companion, Dr. Bat, who on the dark prairie misidentified Asinus as a horned, carnivorous quadruped, commented, "I was silly enough to mistake my own faithful beast for a monster. Though even now I greatly marvel to see this animal running at large."

When I was a child I marveled to see them, as well, but now I viewed their presence at Custer as a mockery, a hairy insult to a place that, despite the name, was still a shrine to the once immense, almost extinct prairies. The proper habitat of such creatures, it seemed to me, was a petting zoo or a western pulp novel or a Frankie Laine song: *My mule and I, we haven't a care.* Careless—that seemed to sum it up perfectly. Here was a species that had been the careless instrument of the careless American exploration, settlement, and mining of this land, stolen from its rightful inhabitants. This particular herd, I'd read somewhere, was descended from burros that had once hauled tourists to the top of Harney Peak—yet another place named for a prolific Indian killer—and then been carelessly relocated here, to beg and breed in the heart of this magnificent prairie park.

Not that they weren't appreciated by some. During our vacation in 1975, my parents bought a small TV-shaped viewfinder for my sisters and me, for which we thanked them by fighting over it the rest of the trip. If you held the TV up to the light, you could see seven "prominent" features of South Dakota, including Dinosaur Park, the Corn Palace, Mount Rushmore, a stagecoach—and the burros of Custer State Park! The "World Famous" crucifixion of Christ didn't make the cut, but the burros did. Just another example, I thought, of Midwesterners carelessly celebrating the destruction of what had once made their homeland unique. In my own state of Iowa, in the early nineteenth century, civic leaders stood witness to a tallgrass wilderness, to a diversity of life that rivaled the rain forest. But when it came time to choose a nickname for their new state, instead of honoring that remarkable natural heritage, they chose instead to honor Hawkeye, the popular literary character who despised it.

Asses, indeed, I thought, and blared the horn.

I was glad to leave the burros behind and enter the borders of Wind Cave National Park, a place at least named for a natural feature, though still not prairie—the vertical landscape, even subterranean, continued to claim center stage. The parking lot near the cave entrance was full, as it had been nearly twenty

years ago. The cave is a remarkable place, and I remembered being intrigued by the story of how, in 1881, two brothers hunting in the area had heard a strange whistling and followed it to a
small opening in the earth. That hole led to an extraordinary
cave complex, containing miles of tunnels, underground pools
and streams, massive stalactites. I marveled at all of it during
our visit there, especially the idea that anywhere, underneath
what I might have thought to be familiar ground, there could be
a secret, fantastic realm that would take a lifetime to explore.
Our pregnant mother hadn't been as thrilled with the tour. At
one point, as we descended, she became woozy and had to sit
down, and perhaps it was that, or the stratified layers of the
earth itself, that caused time to reassert itself in my imagination.
The tour guide had explained that we were not merely descend-
ing through space, but through millions of years. As Dad sat
with his arm around Mom, his voice burdened by what I
thought might be fear, I had wondered if somewhere in this
earth, here or elsewhere in the Hills, there were artifacts from as
far back as my parents' honeymoon, clues to who they'd been,
what they'd thought and felt back then. That unimaginable
stretch of time when none of us had been born or lost.

I continued past the cave and into the surrounding grasslands. For the first time during that trip, I missed the compan-
ionship of others. I missed Stephanie, who couldn't come along
because of her teaching job. Since my first awakening to the
prairies during the floods, two years before, she'd become my
frequent companion on journeys to discover and explore what
remained of the native grasslands. She'd even helped harvest
seeds for a prairie restoration near Des Moines, an experience

that she claimed had moved her toward a new love for this mountainless region, a new sense of being at home. If she had joined me on this trip to the Black Hills, would it have deepened her love for this land, even our love for each other, as it had for my parents? I missed my parents, as well, and my sisters—the sweet intensity of a young family exploring a few of the wonders of the world. Would I someday bring children of my own here? I spotted a solitary bison bull ambling across the grass, pulled the car over to the side of the road, and took out my camera. Peering through the telescopic lens, I discovered that the bull wasn't alone, that there was a pronghorn in the near distance, blending with the grass. While capturing that moment, that vertical still-life—hills, grass, pronghorn, bison— I felt yet another absence. Somewhere in the space between that wild scene and my eye, there might have been another companion on this journey. Two young men, instead of one, growing up together, finding their way into the prairies, finding their way back home.

I grabbed my pack, which included (this time) a compass and plenty of water but not the kerosene stove, and marched across the prairie. It displayed a brilliance of color, a vastness, which made Custer State Park seem constricted. The grasses were in fall glory, the rich russet of the little bluestem, splashed with golden nests of buffalo grass, blue grama, needle-and-thread. There were plenty of invasive species to be found, but the ponderosa and junipers, so thick elsewhere in the Hills, had mostly retreated due to controlled fires and clearings. The place was loud with birdsong—meadowlarks, warblers—and a goshawk shot across the sun and over a distant ridgeline. My eyes rested on that elevation before returning to the open terrain, where perspective was more difficult, where space seemed, at times, dimensionless. This is what Albert Pike meant, I think, when he said the prairie throws a man back on himself, to find orientation, but it is a self strangely empty of ego, free of the obvious and usual goals—no mountain peak, no sandy bottom of a subterranean pool. No future happiness or security to attain, no past mistakes or sorrows. Only the journey, which is endless. This is another enduring deception of the prairies, what earlier explorers and pioneers found so foreign and horrifying, what sometimes drove them mad. It is also, I think, one of its enduring mercies.

I followed in that direction for I don't know how long, until I heard a strange noise on the breeze—a deep whistling scream. I followed it, because following strange whistling noises in that country can lead to unexpected treasures. A mile or so later, the bottom of the prairie dropped away, revealing a hidden, dusk-shadowed valley. Another whistling scream emerged from the branches of a dead oak, which appeared—Was I hallucinating?—to tip, twist, and dance. Then I saw the head, the eyes, the vague outline of a massive body through the grass, and realized it was a reclining bull elk, the tree his antlers, much closer than I realized. The elk's head tilted back to release another high-pitched, throaty bugle, which was answered by another bull making his way into the valley from the opposite side. And then another, much louder, from a tree-encrusted hillside where he and his extended family of elk cows and calves were ensconced. I was witnessing for the first time a challenge, a heated conversation that had been taking place on those grasslands for millennia. This was, in fact, the first time I'd seen wild elk roaming their native prairies. Their species, like the grizzly bear and the cougar and the wolf, had been mostly chased into the private, rarefied air of the mountain West until those elevations came to seem the definition of their home, their identities. Now here they were and I watched them in awe, losing self and time once again, until the hastening dusk encouraged me to find a spot to camp. I stretched out in my sleeping bag, beneath the brightening stars, and fell asleep.

It's tempting to end the story here—the fool redeemed, the wild dreams come true. It would have ended here if I hadn't felt compelled, the next morning, to return to Custer State Park. Along the Wildlife Loop, I drove without stopping past the prairie dog town, the bison, a gathering of pronghorn, and parked along the stretch of road claimed by that strange and unexpected prairie species *Asinus domesticus Americanus*. They inevitably approached and surrounded the car, and after a moment's hesitation, I rolled down both windows and offered up what was left of my breakfast: two apples, a banana and several oatmeal bars. They stuffed their heads through both sides to get at the food, and those that weren't as lucky or aggressive covered my windshield with a complimentary film of saliva, which had a surprisingly corrosive effect on the bug guts. I knew I was probably breaking some rule of the park, of the proper relationship to animals in the wild, but who was going to tell? I was alone in the land of deception and loss, willing to pay for a little of their unapologetic honesty, their unbridled desire—begging in the midst of a once plentiful place, now dependent on the mercy of others to sustain and protect it. The bison and the elk, in their aloof grandeur, seemed above such displays, though they were no less dependent on them. Here was the naked need of a nation, as well, that had long considered the prairies the ultimate reservoir of its dreams and desires: for riches, for Eden, for a new start. A nation that included my pioneer ancestors, my immigrant great-grandmother and my parents, who'd come here to forge their love and, later, to help forge a new future as a family, beyond grief.

Then there were my own needs and desires, to redeem the past, to discover and solidify a new self, a kinship with the wild prairies. As another googly-eyed, slobbering burro pressed its head through the window, I reconsidered my earlier judgment of them. This was one moment, perhaps not the best, in their hopefully long donkey lifetime on the prairie. What I'd experienced here, for a few moments, was the burros' everyday reality—observing the herds of bison and elk in the still dawn air, resting with their burro siblings in the cool of deep grass, beneath fire-hot afternoons, nestling their young under the stars. Witnessing the yearly renewal of this land where, just down the road, beyond their knowledge or care, a human Christ is regularly crucified and resurrected. What must they think of themselves? How far had they come from their days as the "hack," the dumb instrument, the slave of progress that had once dragged careless tourists up the steep slopes of Harney Peak— the place the Oglala holy man, Black Elk, had once called the "center of the world"? The place where he had gone to confront the disappointment of his own desires—for his people, for his homeland, for himself. Had the ancestors of these burros been witness to that defining human moment as well? Did they continue to bear witness as countless others fled to this park, these hills and grasslands, to confront their desires—to confront desire itself? The fiery center that, as it does the prairie, burns and renews all creation.

Whether there was such a flame in the bulging, expectant eyes of those burros, I can't remember. Only that in looking into them, I saw my own.

SHOVELING

—⊷⊶—

Steph wakes me at an unfamiliar hour. It's 6:30 in the morning and it has snowed. "It's our turn to shovel," she says, as I try to bury my face in the pillow. We alternate shoveling duties with our downstairs neighbors, and up until today we've managed to be out of town during snowstorms. Oh well, we rationalized, they have teenagers who need to earn their allowance. This time there's no escape. Steph leaves for work as I stumble to the dresser to find the long johns.

Outside, the frigid air pulls the warmth right out of my underwear. Because there is nothing but open fields to the northwest, the arctic winds travel an easy channel to our front door. The drifts on the sidewalk are more than three feet deep, despite just a few inches of actual snowfall. It's hard not to admire the way the early dawn's light lingers on its surface, softening contours, making it appear more natural and familiar than the solid slope of earth it covers. A new world, born this morning. I'm reluctant to disturb it.

The silence is interrupted by my next-door neighbor, Mike, who is zipped into his yellow snowmobile suit and dragging his snow blower out of the garage. He and his wife, Ruth, have been especially friendly to us since we moved to Belle Plaine. They've treated us to dinner for our anniversary, let us grow vegetables in a section of their garden, and invited us to sit on their deck and watch the satellites pass overhead. When they heard I was interested in prairie, they took us to a nearby Odd Fellows cemetery, overgrown with native grasses and wildflowers.

"Don't worry," Mike calls out. "I'll clear that front sidewalk for you after I'm done with the home." Mike runs the funeral home across the street, like his father and grandfather before him. He was born in this small town, and was raised in the rooms above the family business. Although he and his family now live in the ranch house next to ours, Mike seems most himself while setting up Christmas angels or trimming the yew hedges in front of that bright two-story home across the street, where, from time to time, the community gathers to mourn and remember. Steph and I admire his deep roots.

"Thanks," I reply, "but it looks like you have enough work already." The drifts in their driveway look twice as high as those that roll out before me and, catching the full gold of the rising sun, twice as beautiful.

Two years ago, in 1993, Steph and I decided to move to Belle Plaine because it was halfway between her teaching job in the small town of Dysart and Iowa City, where I'm still attending graduate school and working as a teaching assistant. That first evening, our moving van parked in front of the Victorian house where we are still renting, in the middle of a torrential downpour—one of many during that summer of the floods. My sisters, Carrie Anne and Susan, as well as my future brother-in-law, Mark, and my German friend, Elmar, made the trip with us. Even with all that help, we somehow managed to lodge the couch between two interior doorways, where it remained stuck for several days, floating in midair, until we relented and borrowed a saw. There were other unusual sights during those first weeks in Belle Plaine: The bodies of hundreds of dead frogs scattered on our sidewalk. The transformation of the cornfield across the street into a wetland, where we watched redwings and killdeer and coots and pelicans and little blue herons with their ivory-feathered young. The prairie reawakening in nearby ditches. Here was a place that, as today, under the snow, defied all expectation.

I step my way around the house, through the thigh-high drifts, to the back shed, where I keep the shovel. It's cheap and flimsy, with a blade like crumpled aluminum foil. I worry it may not make it through another workout. But when I plunge into the first drift and easily toss the light, crystalline flakes, there's no problem. I finish the back driveway, the front stairs, and the sidewalk in less than an hour.

I'm feeling so good, I start shoveling Mike's sidewalk as well. Halfway through, a wind picks up, and suddenly the air is a flurry of movement, the flakes migrating up and down, away and back again. I have to pull up my scarf to keep my frozen lips from falling off and joining them. I think affectionately of the spring to come. If it's anything like the other springs here, I'll be able to look out the second-story window by my desk and see red-tailed hawks floating above the fields, as if attached to kite strings. I'll see small flocks of mallards flap their way toward Otter Creek Marsh, just over the Bohemian Hills. Sometimes, if

I bend my neck and peer deeper into the sky, I'll glimpse the soaring sliver of a bald eagle. Tomcats, perhaps the orange tiger and the gray, will be moving through the neighborhood, on the lookout for wary Juliets. Robins will be everywhere and wasps will return to dust off their paper nests near the eaves. I miss them all.

Among the human population, the retirees, or "snowbirds," will return from winter homes in Arizona and Florida to get reacquainted with their growing grandchildren, who will be bursting through the neighborhood park and racing along this same sidewalk on bicycles and skateboards. Mike's teenage son will finally be riding his new motorcycle around the block, instead of just revving it up in the driveway. The rumble and hoot of the Chicago & North Western Railroad will be more frequent, as will be the hiss of cars on Highway 30, part of the historic Lincoln Highway, "Main Street to America." At some point during the summer we will follow that highway across the plains and into the Great Basin, on our way to visit Steph's family in Idaho. We'll stay in cheap motels, look forward to eating in small cafés, and inevitably get stranded in some hot, unexpected place like Rock Springs.

At the moment, standing in the deep snow, my only option is to travel across the street, which is what I do after finishing Mike's sidewalk. I want to invite him to join me for breakfast at the downtown Lincoln Café, but he's nowhere to be found. I walk to the back of the funeral home and finally spot him nearly two blocks away, pushing his blower along the sidewalk, shooting the snow into the street in a giant, arcing fountain. A woman with white hair watches him from her front porch.

I start walking the four blocks to the café alone, as I've done many times before. The street is more crowded than usual. I stop to listen to a man complain about sloppy snowplow drivers, chase our landlord's wayward border collie through the park and back to their house, and help a teenager push his car out of a snowdrift. At the corner of the main intersection, I greet a retired, elderly priest outside his residence in the historic hotel, where he manages a laundromat in the basement. He has decorated the dank walls of that facility, which we visit weekly, with paintings of saints and Republican presidents, and countryside prints by Currier and Ives—all of which has led me to make a few unpleasant judgments about him. I guess I have a problem with politicians, of any party, sharing the same wall space with saints and Currier and Ives.

As it turns out, though, the priest is about to check on some local shut-ins, and has a lot to tell me about the plight of the poor in rural areas.

"We must all do what we can, yes?"

"Yes," I say, and am reminded of what little I know about him, and about the place in which we live.

During the years since that first, flooded summer in Belle Plaine, Steph and I have been slow to enter the rhythms of the community. Our distant jobs leave us little time in town and it's our hope that during the next couple of years I'll finish grad school and find a tenure-track teaching position at a university, which will mean moving once again. I will turn thirty this summer and, looking around, I see people my age who are already merging into the fast lane of upward mobility, ticking off miles of credit and ordering items from a more lucrative drive-through menu: a house, a nice car, mutual funds. In contrast, we pay rent and try, unsuccessfully, to figure out why the horn on our rusted Prelude keeps going off in the middle of the night, in subzero weather. We're ready to move on, toward more security, perhaps toward parenthood, the adventurous terrain of family where we will hopefully chase our own children across neighborhood parks.

At the café, I stomp the snow off my boots, slump down in the nearest seat and open the local newspaper. It's filled with articles about school and social events, the always precarious farm economy, ice-fishing contests, church functions, births, funerals, weddings. It makes me regret the fact that, in our impatience, Steph and I have tended to treat Belle Plaine as more of a pause than a real home. We seek out natural scenery, not social commitment, and we sleep in on Sundays. Our harried schedules normally drown out any feelings of isolation and allow us to move unaware through our daily life in this place. But this morning, having watched Mike drag his blower toward his familial home, and other neighbors whose names I still don't know emerge to shovel and chat with one another, or to help those in need, I feel the separation.

"Decaf again, hon?" The waitress is standing over me with the coffeepot.

"Thanks," I reply, holding out my cup, surprised she remembers what kind of coffee I prefer. Surprised she remembers me at all.

Tonight, after our supper of boxed macaroni-and-cheese, Mike drops by with a plate of warm prune kolache. He says his Bohemian neighbor, Irene—the woman with the white hair—makes them on snow days to thank him for clearing her sidewalk, just as she did for his father. Now, to thank me for clearing his walk, he is passing a dozen or so on to us. The gesture catches us off guard, and Steph darts to the kitchen to get another jar of homemade salsa from the summer garden. It's our first attempt at canning— the last jar we gave them contained floating clumps of coagulated corn starch, which we'd mistakenly used as a thickener.

"No, no," he says. "Just enjoy and I'll see you tomorrow morning. Don't go anywhere—it's supposed to snow again tonight."

We follow him downstairs to the porch and, waving and babbling thanks, watch him walk to his deck, where I hope, in the spring, we will sit and watch satellites together, as well as the arrival of Comet Hyakutake—the "dirty snowball"—as it migrates through space at over a hundred thousand miles per hour. It will be a spectacular sight, I'm sure, but at the moment I don't envy its motion. I think we may be moving fast enough.

Mike closes his door and Steph and I are alone again, in the cold. It's silent and dark except for the window lights scattered along the street. It has started snowing again, as predicted, and the falling crystals make the lights flicker like isolated campfires in a prehistoric landscape. They join with the lights of the next block and the next to create a winding path that leads away to the west, levitates, then vanishes over the crest of the distant and invisible Bohemian Hills.

As we turn to go inside, I look forward to tomorrow's dawn, when we will all be united, once again, by the generosity of the sky.

PART THREE

Home

DAVE AND THE DEVIL

—◦◦—◦◦—

My cousin Dave wondered if showing the video of a voodoo priestess eating a live rooster had been a mistake. It was March 1998, and he and I were sitting conspicuously alone together in the college cafeteria. Dave's seminar students, most of them health professionals from this small Iowa community, were gathered at various other tables, whispering and flashing us looks that ranged from curious to indignant. None of them were eating chicken. I tried to assure Dave that, if anything, the timing of the video had been unfortunate (coming just before lunch break) but had otherwise served as a dramatic climax to his lecture on the history of satanism and the occult.

"I'm not that worried," he shrugged. "This audience is pretty tame. In Wisconsin, a group of satanists attending my seminar spent the whole time chanting and trying to throw a spell on me. Now that was interesting."

It was also gutsy, I thought. Dave was in his late twenties, as tall, blond, and muscular as Dolph Lundgren, towering over me even while sitting in his chair. As owner and president of Cornerstone Seminars, he'd spent the last few years traveling to do consulting work on cults and satanism, as well as on gangs and "student-initiated violence," and to present educational seminars to everyone from church groups to teachers to police detectives. In 1993, he'd bought the business from Dr. William Reisman, retired minister and ex-college professor, who'd founded Cornerstone in 1989 and still helped Dave with his increasingly overbooked schedule. Together, they might have been considered part of what one sociologist referred to as a "growing number of self-styled 'occult experts' [who] make the rounds on the TV and radio talk shows and earn a living as lecturers and consultants." Unlike many of these experts, however, Cornerstone (based in Indianola, Iowa) had earned a serious regional and even national reputation. During the previous year, in 1997, they'd been hired on the recommendation of the FBI as consultants to educators, police, and town officials in Pearl, Mississippi, where a high school student had been accused of cult-related murders. Dave had provided similar consultation in West Paducah, Kentucky, where a fourteen-year-old boy had opened fire at a school prayer meeting, killing eight. Later that month, he would give a presentation to the Drug Enforcement Administration in Kansas City, and in June, at the request of Pearl mayor, Jimmy Foster, he would conduct a day-long debriefing on student-initiated violence for public administrators and other professionals from affected communities around the nation.

To these people David Price represented a wealth of practical, objective knowledge that had helped calm individual fears, debunk conspiracy theories, and, in the words of Mayor Foster, "channel our city's emotions in a positive, factual direction." To

me, though, he was just Dave and the situation we found ourselves in at the cafeteria table was an all-too-familiar one. Dave
is a couple of years younger than me and grew up in Spencer, a
small industrial city in northwest Iowa. During our awkward
teenage years, when both our towns were suffering from the
farm crisis, he and I became irresistibly drawn to the macabre.
We often spent family visits alone together in a corner with our
black and red pencils concocting comic book tales of vampires
and zombies and killer snapping turtles and subterranean gargoyles trying to take over the world. We discussed like scholars
the latest installments of *Halloween* and *Friday the 13th* and *Psycho,* and hungrily perused the blood-soaked pages of his *Fangoria* magazines. Our fascination perplexed and sometimes
infuriated our parents, but it also forged a unique bond between
us. I was attending his seminar, in part, because of that bond.

I was also there—though I hadn't told Dave this yet—to get
his advice on a very real case of animal mutilation that had recently happened near the isolated Iowa farmhouse Steph and I
were renting. We'd moved there from Belle Plaine, closer to the
university where I'd been hired as a low-paid visiting adjunct
professor—a temporary appointment while I continued to
search for a tenure-track job. The victim was a stray cat, which
I'd discovered beheaded and disemboweled beside the log pile.
Normally, I would've dismissed it as the work of predators, except
I was afraid this might be the work of one of Steph's middle-
school students. This student, Mitchell—a squatty kid who
painted his lips and fingernails black and listened to Marilyn
Manson music—had publicly proclaimed himself to be a fol-
lower of "the Dark Lord." He had also proclaimed his hatred for

Steph, one of the few teachers at her new school who'd consistently disciplined him for his disruptive behavior. Until recently, his defiance of Steph had been limited to name-calling, but then the previous month he'd loudly bragged to his friends that he was going to "liquidate" her. Though Mitchell's father was in prison, school officials were downplaying his behavior as that of a typically rebellious, attention-starved teenager. We were angry about this, and afraid. It was the late nineties and still pre-Columbine, but there'd been all those other school shootings to feed our growing paranoia. I was hoping Dave's seminar would either calm my fears or give me something substantial that I could use to convince school officials, possibly even the police, to permanently remove the kid from my wife's presence.

"Well, I'm sure we all had an enjoyable lunch," Judy said after we returned to the classroom, provoking a few guffaws. Judy was the coordinator of continuing health education at the community college, and she'd first heard of Cornerstone on the news program *48 Hours*. She'd hired Dave to give a five-hour seminar on "Satanism and the Occult: Fact versus Fiction" to this group of nurses, social workers, emergency medical staff, and hospital administrators. The advertised intent had been to familiarize them with the physical signs of ritual abuse, but so far Dave had focused on what he called "the background," including an abbreviated history of satanism (from Aleister Crowley to Anton LaVey), a list of differences between religious satanism and secular (or "freestyle") satanism, and a brief summary of other occult traditions such as Santeria (hence, the rooster video). I was interested in this stuff, but some in the audience had looked impatient, even annoyed. Dave must have sensed this, because after Judy sat down, he immediately launched into the differences between ritual and traditional child abuse, profiled a typical perpetrator and victim, and distributed handouts portraying symbols frequently burned, carved, or tattooed on the bodies of such victims. Everyone was now engaged and taking notes.

Then he closed the blinds.

"To illustrate some of the things I've talked about, I'm going to show a few slides."

Everyone stopped scribbling and I braced myself for another rooster episode. The opening slides were relatively tame: mostly photos of T-shirts, album covers, and wall posters popular with satanic dabblers. There was a photo of Marilyn Manson—Mitchell's favorite—and though I'd already assumed this, I was relieved to hear Dave confirm that Manson was in no way connected to murderous cults. Another photo pictured the seventies musical group Coven, who'd recorded the well-known antiwar anthem "One Tin Soldier." This same group had performed and recorded a satanic mass on an earlier album, a portion of which Dave played on his boom box. This was a bit of a shocker. In high school, after I'd been selected to attend Iowa's Model United Nations, my mother had given me a cassette of "One Tin Soldier" to take to the convention. "As the ambassador from Byelorussia," she'd said, "I hope this song will remind you to be a peacemaker, like the Mountain People." Dave, however, thought the message was closer to Number 7 of the "Nine Satanic Statements" found in *The Satanic Bible*, which he read to the seminar: "Satan represents man as just another animal, sometimes better, more often worse than those that walk on all-fours, who, because of his 'divine spiritual and intellectual development,' has become the most vicious animal of all!"

"So what that song may really be saying," Dave continued, "is that you should literally 'go ahead and hate your neighbor, go ahead and cheat a friend.' To do otherwise, according to satanic principle, is both hypocritical and unnatural."

Dave then moved to the more disturbing photos. The first was of a Baphomet, or "goat's head" pentagram, carved into a teenager's forearm. Dave revealed that, like most of the photos, this one had been taken by Bill Reisman or himself during one of their "investigations" in Iowa or elsewhere in the Midwest—a region that, contrary to arcadian stereotypes, was the very hotbed of satanic activity in this country. There were two factors, he claimed. One: People in the Midwest often grow up among several generations in their family, which allows for more control, secrecy, and abuse within cults. Two: The Midwest is in the Bible Belt, which means adolescents are more likely to rebel or seek attention by defying their parents' traditional religious beliefs. Cornerstone did more business in the Midwest than anywhere else, he said, usually at the behest of local school and city administrators or police. Dave emphasized, however, that most of the occult activities they'd investigated were sporadic and amateurish—not the grand conspiracies envisioned by some—but they'd found things worthy of concern. He ran through several more slides: a teenager's pact with Satan written in blood, a homemade electric chair, and a desecrated mausoleum where someone's skull had been removed.

"That skull might go for five hundred to six hundred dollars on the black market," he said, and I was surprised to see several people scribble the figure in their notebooks.

When we got to the animal mutilations I reached for my own pen. As the distressing images flashed before us—far worse than the rooster—I tried to take notes on the type, location, and potential symbolism of the mutilations. None of them corresponded to the injuries to the dead cat near our log pile, which might've been the work of predators after all. This was welcome information I could take back to Steph, though I was a little disappointed the cat could no longer be used as evidence against Mitchell. I was still not convinced he wasn't a threat, and those fears amplified when Dave showed photos of the bedrooms of teenage cult members. Those bedrooms mostly included innocuous items like red sex candles, Ouija boards, and satanic diaries, but some of them also included ritualistic daggers, hangman's nooses, and guns. Almost all of them were located in the Midwest. After several more slides, and despite Dave's insistence that he was not an alarmist, I was feeling undeniably alarmed by his portrait of our home region. Had this stuff been going on in Fort Dodge, in Belle Plaine, right under my nose? If Dave's claims were true, what was it about the heartland that bred these sorts of behaviors and beliefs? Maybe, as he'd said, they were due to the closely knit generations and large numbers of fundamentalist Christians, but wasn't that also characteristic of the rural South or New England? Was it that, per capita, the Midwest had more domestic animals readily available for sacrifice? More basement bedrooms? More screwed-up teenagers? Or (and I winced at the melodrama) was there something darker at work here?

Apparently, I wasn't alone in wondering these things. When Dave turned on the lights and invited questions, no one asked about ritual abuse. Instead, a woman asked Dave why there were so many slides from her hometown: "Of all the places in Iowa you've investigated, would you say that my town has the most satanists?" When Dave replied that there had indeed been an unusual amount of activity there, several hands shot up, each wanting to know if he'd uncovered something similar in their hometowns. When Dave answered affirmatively, they'd nod and talk in hushed tones to their neighbors, their voices carrying a mix of concern and suspicion—and what I thought might be pride. For a moment, I imagined a host of new welcome signs appearing throughout the state: *Welcome to Dexter: Gateway to Eternal Damnation! Stay in Sloan: Satan's Second Hometown! Bewitching Bondurant: Come Get Burned!*

"I've got to wrap up," Dave announced, "but if you're interested in finding out more about satanism in this region, I'd invite you to attend an upcoming debate at Drake University between my business partner Bill and the self-proclaimed High Priest of Satan in Iowa. Thank you for inviting me, and take care."

When I heard this about Iowa having its very own High Priest of Satan, I decided I had to see this guy—*Would he be wearing a Hawkeye T-shirt and a widow's peak?*—rationalizing that he might shed further light on the Mitchell situation. I waited for the small crowd surrounding Dave to dissipate so I could ask him for more details, but he was preoccupied with an attractive blond who'd requested a copy of Cornerstone's "A Practical Guide to Combat Satanism." When Dave handed her the thin, blood-red text, she handed him a check with her phone number circled at the top.

"Call me when you're in town," she said, and Dave actually blushed.

A week later, back on the farm, I got a phone call. "It's all set," Dave said, clearly excited. "The high priest I told you about, the one who's going to debate Bill, has invited us to attend his next graveyard ceremony. Bill doesn't want to go, but I do—it'll be the first time I've seen a satanic service in person. It's very rare that outsiders get invited. Do you want to come along?"

"Are you kidding?" I said. "I'd love to!"

Dave explained that he'd first heard from this high priest (whom I'll call Jeremiah) after Bill had been interviewed on local television. Jeremiah left a "furious" message on Dave's answering machine, claiming they'd misrepresented the Church of Satan by lumping it in with renegade cults that participate in torture and sacrifices. He insisted true satanists do not participate in such things. That's when Bill called him and set up the debate at Drake. Dave subsequently met with Jeremiah and discovered he was a native Iowan in his late twenties, the son of strict Lutheran parents, and that he'd turned to satanism when he was a teenager. He still lived in his parents' basement, but didn't sport a widow's peak. Dave also found out that during his initial anger with Cornerstone, Jeremiah had put a curse on him and Bill. He'd since removed the curse, but warned Dave that his "children" might not be so forgiving. That was the reason Jeremiah had invited Dave to the ceremony, to educate him and also smooth things over with the coven "before anyone gets hurt."

It struck me, when we hung up, that this excursion might be a little scarier than anticipated. Steph, who'd been listening to my end of the conversation, was even more concerned. Attending a public debate was one thing, she said, but going to an actual ceremony was quite another. She strongly discouraged it, insisting I'd not only be legitimizing Jeremiah's behavior, but might draw unwanted attention to myself, as well as to her and the cats.

"Think about it, John—we live on a farm in the middle of nowhere without a gun. Sound familiar? Did you pay attention at all during those eighties horror flicks?"

She was actually right about the farm—an inordinate number of Dave's slides had been taken inside abandoned barns and farmhouses. I didn't tell Steph this. Instead, I tried to convince her that this guy and his followers were totally harmless—probably just into smelly candles and Black Sabbath—and again rationalized that I might get important insights into her student Mitchell's behavior. Steph wasn't convinced, and neither was I. The truth was I couldn't tell her why I wanted to attend that thing, because I wasn't sure myself.

Dave didn't help my cause when, a few days later, he left this message on our machine: "Dr. Price, this is Will Schreeck from the Foundation of Death. I got your message about needing some ritualistic altar supplies for the upcoming ceremony. A skull is probably going to run you about five hundred dollars. I can get you some candles made from human fat for about a hundred and ten to a hundred and fifty, depending. Either of these gifts will greatly please those in attendance, but if you're looking for something less expensive, I suggest you bring one of your cats. Thanks and have a happy Sabat."

I found this humorous, but Steph thought Dave might be nuts, and that I was dangerously naïve and—given my stressed-out condition—ripe for cult-style brainwashing.

"By the time your little adventure is over," she told me, voice shaking, "I wouldn't be surprised if these people have you trained to axe-murder all of us at the sound of the phone ringing! You have to promise me you *will not* attend this thing!"

I promised, then made plans to meet Dave for lunch.

"If I didn't have a sense of humor about some of this stuff, I really would go nuts," Dave said. We were sitting in the coffee shop beneath his apartment/office in Indianola. I told him that Steph was a bit sensitive about her situation at school. Actually, we were both sensitive about it. I told him about Mitchell.

"Threats are always a concern," he said, "but I don't think she has anything to worry about. First of all, you say the kid is popular and these shootings almost always involve kids who are isolated from their peers. Second, he hasn't done anything I didn't do at that age—Remember my bedroom?"

I recalled that Dave's adolescent bedroom had been in the basement, and that it had indeed resembled many of those featured in his slides. It was a dark, windowless space with faux wood paneling that he'd covered with horror movie posters, the largest being the guy in the human skin mask from *The Texas Chain Saw Massacre*. The low ceiling was plastered with cutouts of heavy-metal bands such as Iron Maiden and Quiet Riot and others who liked to pose in spiked dog collars and straitjackets. There was a dead crow attached, with wire, to his headboard. Dave's parents had refused to install a door for the room (a blessing, he now says), so he hung strings of orange and black beads to create a voodooish portal. During family visits to Spencer, I'd usually been the only one willing to cross that portal to spend time alone with him. Dave would crank up a KISS song, break out the *Fangoria* magazines, and invite me to eat a cold hotdog using the decorative machete his dad had purchased on vacation in Mexico.

I loved that bedroom, probably for reasons similar to Dave's. I was short and pimply in early adolescence while Dave was chubby and had a lazy eye. Neither of us was popular or excelled in sports, which was especially hard on Dave, being a coach's kid. Dave eventually experienced a prodigious and (for our family) unprecedented growth spurt—six foot four or five—and became the starting defensive end for his high school football team. He told me at the coffee shop, however, that he'd never stopped feeling isolated and resentful. Throughout high school and college he'd continued to crave attention and power, and those feelings had led to an almost uncontrollable desire to scare people in authority, especially teachers. Once, for a school composition assignment—about the same time I was concocting my own comic book horror tales—he'd written an illustrated story about a demon named Helmet Head Harry who emerged from an old farmer's well, wrapped his flaming tongue around people's necks, and bashed their heads against his rock-hard skull until their brains flopped out. His mother wasn't the only one back then who thought he needed counseling.

"One of my high school teachers came to a seminar I gave in Spencer and couldn't believe it was me," Dave said. "He told me that when I was in school he'd worried that I was into cults and drugs. I told him, 'That's exactly what I wanted you to think.'"

I asked Dave how he'd gotten involved with Bill and Cornerstone Seminars, and he said it was just dumb luck. At Simpson College, Dave had been a few months from graduating with a Criminal Justice degree when he discovered, to his real horror, that he was one credit hour short. He asked his adviser if there was an easy internship available for credit, and she mentioned a local guy who lectured on cults and satanism. Dave immediately signed up. When he arrived at Bill's office he expected to do some collating, get his one credit, and move on. But that same week in February happened to be the beginning of the siege at the Branch Davidian compound in Waco. Dave helped research the criminal/cult profile Bill sent to the FBI, warning them that the standoff would probably end in mass suicide. According to Dave, the FBI ignored their report, but when all those people died inside the burning compound, Cornerstone gained the FBI's attention and respect. Bill also gained Dave as a business partner.

"I knew that first day that I'd found my calling. I'd been a big partier in college, totally lacking direction, but then this work, I don't know, it just connected with something inside me, something that needed to get out. I don't make much money— I work two other jobs during the week—but without Cornerstone, I'd probably be the groundskeeper at the Spencer golf course, killing gophers or worse."

I asked Dave about the thick file folder in front of him. He said he was preparing for a meeting with a family from Minnesota. The parents suspected their daughter was involved with a satanic cult, and had sent him her "book of shadows"—what some satanists called their diaries. Dave and Bill would evaluate the diary, meet privately with the girl, ask questions, and try to talk her out of getting further involved. Most of their time, however, would probably be spent calming the parents, who, according to Bill, might be the real source of the problem.

"He thinks this is a typical case of a child without strong parental role models," Dave said. "But it may be more serious than that. The daughter has been in the hospital and is a real suicide risk, so Bill's training as a counselor will be essential. Depressed kids like this one don't join satanic cults because they want to worship Satan. They join because they already worship death. That's the ultimate act of control and power, isn't it—kill yourself, end your pain, and emotionally destroy the people who love you? I have a hard time explaining that to right-wing fundamentalists who see Satan in everything. I'm a Christian, like they are, but I don't believe in giving Satan any more credit than he deserves."

"So you believe in Satan?" I asked this half facetiously, but Dave's expression remained serious.

"Well, yes. I suppose I do."

Back on the farm, I began studying for the graveyard ceremony, which I was even more determined to attend, though I knew it would have to be in secret. Dave hadn't received additional details from Jeremiah, but he assumed the ceremony would take place on or near April 30, Walpurgis Night, an ancient pagan fertility celebration coinciding with the planting of crops.

In the meantime, Dave had loaned me several books on devil worship throughout history, which I kept hidden under a sweatshirt in my closet. I read a chapter or two whenever Steph left to run errands. I couldn't find anything that verified Dave's portrait of the Midwest as a hotbed of satanism. Many of the scholars confirmed, however, that the devil, as enemy or ally, had been especially popular among cultures suffering severe transitions. The Midwest remains an ill-defined region, but one thing it has been during recent centuries is transitional. During the 1980s farm crisis, when Dave and I were teenagers, there were rampant rumors of satanic cow mutilations. These rumors weren't limited to the hallways of my high school; they were reported by newspapers across the Midwest and nationally. Although most of the incidents were determined to be the work of natural forces, this news didn't seem to quell the rumors or the fear that informed them—perhaps the same fear that inflamed hallway talk that international conspiracies and racial preferences were the real reason so many parents lost their jobs. I often wondered if that fear, that sense of powerlessness, was one of the consequences of living in the agricultural Midwest. Dan, the farmer who worked the fields surrounding our house, whose family had lived there for generations, had never owned a scrap of earth—all those acres, and the house, were owned by a guy in Seattle who visited once a year.

There were certainly aspects of living on a farm that Steph and I loved: the quiet days, the clear and starry nights, the apple trees from which we made pie after pie. Sometimes, though, when I was sitting alone on the porch, like right then, it didn't take much effort to imagine evil permeating everything. The burning stench of ammonia fertilizer, the silent bird feeder, the squeal of pigs from the nearby feedlot, the gray line of distant housing developments, the ditch the manager would nag me to mow despite what I'd told him about the snakes and rabbits and pheasants taking shelter there. One moment I was admiring the fields in silent reverie, and the next I was holding my glass of water up to the light, feeling the cancer cells growing in my brain. It seemed that every day I saw tractors spreading their poison across the black, gutted earth. If death was what satanists worshipped, there was plenty to be found around there.

I was almost to the point of empathizing with Mitchell when Steph came home with a new story. She was shaking, nearly in tears. That day in class she'd conducted a verb tense exercise and Mitchell had responded by writing, "I have killed you. I am going to kill you. I will kill you." That's it, I told her, I'm calling the police. Steph held my arm and argued that the police would probably say he's just acting out, and even if they didn't, getting Mitchell expelled might not create the safest situation for her. She said she'd shown his paper to the school counselor, who had promised to take it directly to the principal. *Promised?* She said I should let her handle it, but I didn't want to let her handle it. I wanted to do something. For the next few mornings, while Steph was teaching, I neglected my own pile of student composition papers and searched the books Dave had given me, compulsively writing down quotes like this one from Martin Luther King, Jr.: "He who passively accepts evil is as much involved in it as he who helps to perpetuate it. He who accepts evil without protesting against it is really co-operating with it." I had no idea what to do with this quote, or the others, but writing them down felt vaguely like control. It wasn't long, though, before I was lying helpless on the couch while all the general anxieties of my life—a temporary teaching job, no money, the sound of tractors—flooded into the gaunt, black-edged figure of Mitchell.

"You just need to calm down," Dave told me when I called him. He asked a series of questions—*Has Mitchell become reclusive? Has he radically changed his appearance?*—and once again concluded he was not a threat.

"But how do you know that for sure?" I could hear my voice becoming increasingly hysterical. "I mean, this kid is harming Steph *right now,* emotionally, psychologically, and I want him punished for that. I'm to the point where if nothing is done, I'm going to drive over there and yank the punk out of her class myself—You know what I'm saying?"

"Yeah, I know, but you just need to calm down." He encouraged me to attend a seminar he would be giving later that week in a nearby town. He'd be lecturing on student-initiated violence, he said, and could provide me with even more information. I took a deep breath, and told him I'd be there.

The evening of the presentation, I met Dave at his apartment in Indianola. I'd calmed down enough since our last conversation to notice how tired he seemed, and to resist bombarding him with any more questions about Mitchell. As he collected his things, I sat on the couch and stared at the giant map of the Midwest hanging above his desk. It was covered with red tacks where he was scheduled to give seminars or conduct investigations, nearly two per week until the next January. The apartment was small and sparsely furnished, with one entire wall serving as a repository for his many books and videos on the occult. Perched on top of Dave's television were a Simpson College mug, a wilted Gene Simmons dragon mask, and a Valentine from his mother. Dave and I had been mostly out of touch during his college years, but I remembered hearing about the death of one of his best friends, Brad. During that time, Dave had been drinking regularly and heavily for several years. He and Brad (who attended a different college) had planned to go out for another weekend of partying, but Brad, who'd become seriously overweight, wasn't feeling well. So they went out for coffee instead, and decided that Brad's illness might be a sign that they both needed to get their lives back on track. They promised to get together the next weekend, just to talk and hang out. A few days later, Brad suffocated in his sleep due to severe bronchitis.

Dave had never talked with me about his friend's death, but I'd heard that it had traumatized him for a while, that he'd stopped going to class, that he'd suffered through a long and difficult depression. Sitting there, I wondered how closely that death had occurred to his first days at Cornerstone.

Dave's presentation took place in the school cafeteria, where his voice echoed dramatically among the folded tables and towers of plastic lunch trays. The audience was a mix of school administrators, teachers, and students and their parents, who were there, I assumed, because they had similar questions: *Are we safe? What can we do?* At first, Dave's talk did indeed calm my fears about Mitchell. His presentation was more restrained than the last, more focused, and though he ran through the full collection of graphic slides, his emphasis was less on satanism and the occult than on the basics of adolescent psychology. This was a side of Dave I'd never seen.

"Look at your children," he told us. "Do you sense something is wrong? There are the obvious signs, but mostly it's about your own instincts. If you sense a young person is troubled, that he or she needs your help, then they probably do. Talk to them, let them know you're paying attention, so that even if your instincts are wrong, they'll know you care and that they have to answer to someone besides themselves and their friends."

Dave went on to assert that the reasons behind destructive behavior by kids include an overwhelming ego and lust for personal power. "That's why they're so easily sold on unrealistic role models like Michael Jordan," he said, "and on the supposed status of Nike sneakers and on T-shirts that read, *Winning Is Everything!* and *Second Sucks!* Even our politicians and business leaders model this behavior. So why is it so surprising that kids in this culture are attracted to the rebellious, self-centered character of Satan found in stories and music? You toss in clinical depression, social isolation, and inattentive parents, and you may end up with a child who can kill without remorse."

This statement was meant to be demystifying, empowering, but instead I felt another flood of anxiety sweep through me. *Sneakers? T-shirts?* Suddenly, I was floating again in dark, murky skies where the root cause of despair and violence wasn't any specific person or corporation or landscape or choice. It was American culture itself, as well as the massive economic, political, and military machine that sustains it. How exactly can we protect ourselves and our loved ones from that? Wrestling with the question, it didn't take long to sense how easily anxiety could transform itself into anger—not just the bitter congruence of meaning that leads to paranoia and conspiracy theories, but the all-consuming fury one feels when on the verge of losing belief in human agency. When on the verge of losing belief itself.

"So what exactly do you believe in, Mr. Price?" I turned as if the question had been addressed to me, and spotted a collared minister standing in the back of the room. I sensed he was challenging Dave, perhaps attempting to draw him back to the more familiar, comforting dichotomies: Good versus Evil. God versus Satan. Us versus Them. I already found this minister annoying, his condescending tone, and yet, inside my fear, I also wanted Dave to affirm (because I thought he might believe it and I wanted to believe it) that there were battles to be fought against specific opponents. I wanted him to argue that faith—in God, in country, in humanity—was not just a safe and fashionable conceit. I wanted him to argue that it was possible, through that faith, for good people to keep a finger's grip on a still salvageable world.

Dave ruffled his papers on the podium.

"Well, I guess I'm coming from a Christian view, and that means I believe in the power of forgiveness. Many of the kids I counsel have been told all their lives that they can do anything they want, go anywhere they please—some of you young people will read this in your high school graduation cards. I'm here to tell you it isn't true. Your life will likely turn out very differently from what you planned, and you will make mistakes, some of them terrible. Kids in cults and gangs often tell me they've done things for which they can never be forgiven, and I tell them they're wrong, that there's nothing that can't be forgiven. But that's a hard message to sell, because underneath they're dealing with a void in their lives. If there is a devil to be feared, and I believe there is, then that's it, that void—the one we think has to be filled but never will be."

A year later, Dave visited us in western Iowa, where we'd moved after I'd accepted (with much relief) a tenure-track position at the nearby University of Nebraska at Omaha. For the first time in our lives, Steph and I owned the house we lived in—a rickety Victorian located in town. After dinner, while Dave and I sat on the deck gazing into the woods that separated us from a cemetery, I told him that part of my original attraction to the property had been the fact that two different neighbors had told us it was haunted. I found out from the lady who'd lived in the house for most of the twentieth century that the ghost was a man who'd died from asthma in the late 1800s. That was one of the ghost's characteristics, she'd said: He's a wheezer. We had yet to experience this specter or anything else supernatural, but I liked telling the story to Dave.

"Cool," he said.

Earlier that day, at our local hospital, Dave had given another seminar on satanism and the occult, but I hadn't attended. I hadn't attended any of his presentations since the one in the school cafeteria. I hadn't lost interest; I simply had other things on my mind: department committees, home repairs, plans to start a family. The confrontations with evil I'd so anticipated last spring never materialized. High Priest Jeremiah inexplicably backed out of the debate with Bill, and canceled our invitation to the graveyard ceremony. Mitchell never acted on his threats to Steph or to anyone else. Even the neighborhood fascination with our ghost seemed far from the satanic conspiracies that had once tempted my imagination, veering closer instead to the ancient fascination with *genius loci*—the spirit that inhabits and defines a particular place. To be haunted, in other words, may be one of the privileges of settling down.

Dave, however, was far from settled. Since the Columbine murders he'd been traveling throughout the region and beyond, responding to the increasingly urgent question printed in bold on the covers of our national magazines: WHY? Suddenly, the whole country was discussing the challenges of responsible parenting, adolescent depression, and "a youth culture of violence." According to one poll, the majority of Americans believed it was "somewhat or very likely that a shooting incident could happen at their local schools." Dave had been so busy responding to these people's concerns about the future, he'd had virtually no time to consider his own. He lived in the same Indianola apartment, and had yet to fulfill his dream of enrolling in graduate school. Nor had there been an opportunity to start a family or even sustain a long-term relationship. His last girlfriend had ended it when she opened his car trunk to discover a large, blood-spattered voodoo doll that had been given to him by an Iowa police chief.

"I'm not sure why she reacted that way," he said, taking a sip of coffee. "She knew about my work. Maybe it finally started to scare her—hell, it scares me sometime. And speaking of scary, tell me about your woods over there. Have you noticed any suspicious activity—bonfires, animal screams, that kind of thing?"

I was reminded then of how much I liked Dave, and how much I hoped he'd keep doing what he was doing. Soon, how-

ever, the nation would once again turn its eyes outward, intent
on a perceived evil beyond the boundaries of our culture. Dave's
message and expertise would no longer be in high demand; his
business would drop off. He'd retire from Cornerstone, buy an
old house in a small town, and become a mortgage loan officer
and then a school counselor for at-risk kids. He'd fall in love,
marry, and raise children. His efforts, like mine, would then be
thrown into what C. S. Lewis's fictional demon, Screwtape,
claimed to be the more effective crusade against evil: "a hope for
the daily and hourly pittance to meet the daily and hourly
temptation."

Dave and I would return to seeing each other only once a
year or not at all, and I would miss him. Occasionally, at dusk,
after the latest news from our foreign wars, I'd wander alone
onto the deck and find myself anticipating the inevitable day
when we'd return our attention to the devil at home, inside.
When that happens, I hope my cousin is on the front lines. I
hope some evening I'll pick up the phone and hear Dave's voice
inviting me, once again, to be vigilant. To take care. In the familiar woods, the fields, where shadows still play.

Nuts

Several weeks ago I was having a driveway conversation with my neighbor, Todd, when we were interrupted by loud chittering noises. We turned and saw a red fox squirrel chasing a black one up the side of a big bur oak. I told Todd I suspected one of those squirrels was running around inside the walls of our house.

"You know," he replied, "I read somewhere that red squirrels will chew the nuts off black squirrels to keep them from reproducing." Then he walked back to his yard.

I took that as a threat.

This may seem paranoid unless you understand that my neighbor and I are both trying to reproduce and failing. I know this because of other conversations we've had in my driveway. It started just after Steph and I moved into the neighborhood. I was out mending a retaining wall when Todd walked over and said that it sure seemed like hard work and that he wasn't looking forward to terracing the hill in front of his house. He said that if it were up to him, he'd leave the hill alone, but "the wife wants our kids to have a pretty yard with lots of flowers." I said I didn't know he had kids.

"We don't."

"Expecting?"

"Not yet."

He was smiling when he said this, but one year later, Todd has no baby and no terrace. I'd feel sorry for him, except I've been too busy failing to impregnate my own wife. Todd knows this, unfortunately, because of another driveway conversation we had a few months ago. We were shingling the new roof when Todd wandered over to say how good it looked and that he was planning to build an entire second floor on his house to create more room "for the kids." I told him I understood, that that's why we had to get new shingles; rainwater was leaking into "the baby's room." His face fell—"Expecting?"

"Not yet. How about you?"

He shook his head.

I immediately regretted sharing this information with Todd; Steph and I already had enough pressure. Like many of our friends—like Todd and his wife—we'd put off having children until our thirties. We wanted to be settled inside secure jobs; we wanted a house, a yard, a life. The usual reasons. But now that we've decided to have children, we want to have them yesterday. Last winter, Steph and I sat down in the "family room" and came up with a game plan: She would get pregnant in April, the baby would be born in January, and with maternity leave and school vacations we would minimize day care. As each barren month passed we revised the strategy, emphasizing the positive: "Hey, look at it this way, if we conceive next month, the baby will be born in May—Grandpa Roy's birth month!" Now it's October and like the losing football coaches

I'm watching on TV, we've thrown out the game plan. We're in the two-minute offense.

The reproductive process has left me vulnerable in surprising ways—ways I thought were private until Todd's comment about the squirrels. He of all people should have known better than to plant such a troubling image in my head, where it would take root and, later that night, make intimacy more difficult between Steph and me than it should have been. While kissing, I listened to the squirrel scratch around in the walls and wondered, for the first time, if it was a red squirrel or a black squirrel, the aggressor or the victim, the chewer or the chewed. The thought grew, moving down my spinal cord, transforming into an overwhelming sensory experience. No matter where I ran in my mind, I could see it, feel it: the squirrels, the chewing, *the horror.*

The next morning it seemed clear: I had become a victim of sexual sabotage. Todd, my apparently benign neighbor, had drawn first blood in a campaign to prevent me from continuing my genetic line, from succeeding where he had failed. I started imagining counterstrategies. I even did some research at the library, preparing for a future driveway conversation in which I'd be the one launching all the disruptive insights into the natural world. Like, hey, Todd, did you know bull fur seals will lurk offshore until their rivals start copulating and then attack them? Or hey, how about the pungent stink fights between male ring-tailed lemurs? Or hey, have you heard about how the bowerbird likes to demolish the home of his closest sexual competitor? *Why don't you try out those images in the cloacal bed tonight, Todd.*

I've since realized that Todd is not to blame for our failure
to conceive, but at the time it felt better than blaming myself.
Now I'm used to blaming myself. There's no rational reason to
do so: I haven't tested sterile and six months isn't a terribly long
time to try to conceive. Plus I've been weathering reproductive
pressures for years. Shortly after we were married, we were talking casually with friends about having children when their five-
year-old daughter suddenly grabbed my hand and pulled me
over to a pen near their barn. "See," she said, pointing at a pair
of humping pygmy goats, "someday you'll plant a seed in
Stephanie just like Sparky's doing and she'll grow a baby!" I
laughed, of course, as I did when, years later, in the middle of
Wal-Mart, an ex-girlfriend shoved pictures of her kids at me and
asked, "Where's yours?" Or when, at my doctoral graduation,
Grandma Kathryn told me that "smarts don't mean much unless you pass them on." Even when the day finally came, as it
did for Sparky, to plant some seed, the first few months were
lighthearted, providing easy excuses to order pizza, rent French
films, and experiment.

Something changed in September. Steph stepped into the
bedroom doorway and I could tell by her face that we'd failed,
once again. The previous month, on the same occasion, we'd
gone out to a restaurant, eaten fudge sundaes, criticized other
people's bawling kids. Laughed. This time, I spent most of the
night holding her, listening to the sobs, finally understanding
how strung out by hope we'd become. Steph fell asleep, but I
didn't. I went downstairs and out onto the deck. The night was
beautiful—no wind, the moon casting the woods into silver relief. Fireflies sparked in front of a young spruce where I knew a

goldfinch nest was hidden. I'd watched it for weeks, noticing the male at the feeder, peeking at the pale blue eggs, listening to the peeps. The goldfinch—a medieval symbol for the Holy Child, I recalled—had done his job. Now he was probably sound asleep in the spruce, which, at that hour, seemed not so distinct as in the day. It seemed, instead, to have fallen back into the woods, back into the immense tangle of life from which, to my sudden grief, I had somehow become freed. When I crawled back into bed, I put my arm over Steph and whispered the only words that came: *I'm sorry.*

The next morning I wondered aloud what I'd done wrong: *Was it the tight jeans in high school? The pimple medication? Was it too much lying around in front of the television while writing my dissertation? Too much microwave popcorn?* I went on and on until Steph slammed her hand down on the table and told me to knock it off, that it's not my fault. It's nobody's fault. If one of us is sterile or infertile, she said, it's just as likely to be her. Let's wait until we get tested before we panic. Steph was trying hard to be reasonable, I know, but what we felt the night before was beyond reason. It was also, strangely, beyond the circle of our love for each other. I think I realized this for the first time that morning, how the possibility of infertility had thrown us back into ourselves as individuals, John and Steph, male and female, to work through it in our own ways. And over the next few weeks, aside from the late-night sobbing, or maybe because of it, Steph seemed to be working through it better than I. She met with friends, took walks, weeded the garden. In contrast, I avoided people, especially those with children. I also avoided the outdoors, moving quickly from front door to car door to office door. I found that if I lingered too long in the open air, I'd start feeling like the boy in the bubble, convinced that my body was a troubled, poisoned ecology sealed off from the fertile cycles of life around me. In such a state, every bug, every leaf, every wild cry mocks.

After a week or so of intense indoor activity—painting walls, reading, writing—I'd almost convinced myself that I could hide from the outdoors, from the daily reminders of my failure. But then the outdoors came indoors. The squirrel. It dug a hole under the new roof and started scratching around inside our bedroom walls. The first time I heard it, Steph and I were "trying" and it distracted me. Not that it took much. The squeaky bed frame, the dripping faucet, an Alanis Morissette song on the radio—any of these were enough to cause difficulties. But the squirrel was different. By visiting us in that moment, the creature seemed to be flaunting its reproductive prowess, its two litters a year, its ability to mate while hanging onto a tree branch, wrists rotating 180 degrees. I tried to change the mental channel to a different pest, but each time, obscure reproductive facts and the voices of various exterminators surfaced to deflate me. What if the scratching wasn't a squirrel, but a mouse? *Mice can have twelve litters and over eighty young a year.* Roaches? *A roach can get his head cut off and continue mating for a week.* A bird? *In one species, the males have the human equivalent of fifty-pound testes.* It didn't matter—squirrel, mouse, roach, bird—they were all eating away at my home, eating away at the very foundations of my ability to reproduce.

So I gave up hiding indoors and returned to neglected yard work. That's when I had the unfortunate squirrel conversation with Todd, and the weirdness intensified. Over the next few days, I became increasingly worried that Todd would impregnate his wife first, thereby exacerbating our pain and, through that stress, further reducing our chances. When I caught myself watching him and his wife in their front yard, studying them for signs of success—giddy laughter, hand-holding, flower picking—I knew something had to give.

I decided to turn to my closest male friends for advice. I planned to begin by asking them about fertility and then, if it went well, raise the psycho factor. It didn't go well. Most seemed reluctant to talk, hiding behind easy prescriptions like "boxers instead of briefs." In my altered state, I interpreted their reticence as further proof that all men, know it or not, are in genetic competition with each other and cannot be trusted for advice. There were, however, a few who tried to be helpful. One confessed that he and his wife had resorted to artificial insemination. For a guy we had nicknamed "The Mailman" during league basketball games, this confession took guts. His story got me thinking more about the promise of medical miracles. Fertility pills, for instance—maybe we'd end up with septuplets like the McCaugheys and get a free house and minivan from the Iowa governor. At the time, however, I was convinced I could do it on my own, employing more natural remedies like better diet and exercise. But I was still open to suggestions. One friend recommended trimming the hair off the scrotum to keep it cool. This sounded like a risky procedure. And for all I knew, that was his intent.

I'm done talking to men now. I've been talking to God instead, confessing, cutting deals. Late at night, I fill with remorse for the ways I've wasted my body's resources over the years, spilling them randomly and without purpose. I worry this wastefulness has been a kind of sin against God, for which I'm now being punished. So I've been praying for forgiveness. During these prayers, I often recall the televangelist Steph and I stumbled upon a few years ago while channel surfing. The slicked-back preacher was hopping around the stage, spitting on and on about the evils of birth control, including withdrawal. His biblical reference was Genesis 38, Verses 1–10, the story of Onan. God had recently "slewn" Onan's older brother, Er, for crimes unnamed and it had become Onan's duty to sleep with his brother's widow, conceive a son, and preserve Er's patriarchal line. The preacher read, "And Onan knew that the seed should not be his; and it came to pass, when he went in unto his brother's wife, that he spilled it on the ground, lest that he should give seed to his brother." Whatever Onan's secret motives—lust, greed, genetic competition—they "displeased the LORD: wherefore he slew him also."

The message then was laughable: *If I can't conceive a son, will Steph have to sleep with cousin Dave? Should human males, like cats, have penile barbs to prevent early withdrawal?* But during these late nights, the message has returned as a more serious question: Just how closely entwined are the ecologies of body and spirit? Have I, in squandering the fruits of one, squandered those of the other?

Sometimes, though, it helps to think of my reproductive self as a necessary sacrifice, as a rightly poisoned ecology, the demise of which will not be mourned by God or anyone else. On the contrary, it may be worthy of celebration. I recently retrieved two newspaper articles on overpopulation and stuck them to the refrigerator. One was covering the birth of "the world's six billionth child" in Bosnia. The boy and his mother had received a visit from U.N. Secretary-General Kofi Annan which, I thought, probably wasn't as welcome as a new house and minivan would've been. Nevertheless, I was surprised to learn that despite the staggering numbers, world reproductive rates are actually slowing down. *Boston Globe* columnist Jeff Jacoby picked up this fact in the other article, declaring it further proof that humans are the superior animal, that people "don't breed like rabbits, multiplying without regard to their ability to support their offspring." *Right on,* I thought—and that goes for squirrels, too.

But then, in the second half of his column, Jacoby started worrying about an impending "baby bust," and that fewer people in the world would mean fewer minds at work to solve our problems. "For babies are a blessing," he wrote. "And the more babies each generation produces, the more blessed is the generation that follows." I tried to fight back the lump in my throat. I reminded myself that American children aren't like other children in the world, that they gobble up more than their fair share of sugared cereals, petroleum, and trees. I reminded myself that it's easy to choose to have children when your ability to support them is subsidized by starvation half a world away. It's even easier when you believe that your child will grow up to solve the monstrous problems you've created or quietly amplified. This breed of American selfishness makes me hesitant to start handing out blessings to our generation, or the next. Instead, it reminds me of another Bible passage I wish I'd never heard: "Of those to whom much has been given, much will be required." When I think about that one for too long, I fill with fear that God may, in fact, be just.

Still, the article made me sad. Not because of what Jacoby understood, but because of what he did not seem to understand. This thing I'm feeling is not about the next generation or the last. It's about right now, me, my wife, our happiness, our desire to have a child, heaven and earth be damned.

Why do I feel this way?

The question had been frantically knocking around my brain, finding nothing close to an answer. Then, yesterday night, I had a dream. It occurred just after Steph and I—despite the squirrel—had successfully completed our seventh straight day of "trying." I was lying in bed, thinking that I finally understood how rutting elk die from exhaustion, when I drifted into sleep. I woke up in a tree. It was a large tree, with no top or bottom, filled with lots of people, billions of them. They were each holding a ladder that extended way down toward the bottom of the trunk, too far to see. The ladders were wobbly and fragile, but not more fragile than the arms holding them or the faces searching their lengths. I was holding my own ladder, afraid that whatever might latch onto it would be heavy enough to pull me off the branch, but even more afraid that nothing would latch on at all. So I held steady, even as my arms began to tremble and cramp, even as others around me fell or sobbed or shook their empty ladders. Even as they shouted and screamed because they thought they'd seen, just for a second, a small, dimpled hand reach out for them from below.

It had been a while since I'd shared with Steph any feelings or thoughts related to having children, but this morning I told her about the dream. At first she offered a safely scientific interpretation: The ladders are DNA strands, the rungs chromosomes. We're all up the same proverbial tree, trying to extend the genetic line. Then she abruptly got up from the table.

"How did we become so desperate?" she said, and walked out of the room.

Desperate . . . I let the word reverberate through the bowl, the spoon, the bones. Desperate was what I'd been at the junior high dances, skulking along the dark edge of the disco lights, watching girls dance with other boys, wondering if I might ever know the sweet privileges of the flesh. That wasn't who I was now. Or was it? The dream, the feelings, did indeed seem desperate, and despite what I'd thought, they had brought me closer to the natural world. Especially to the squirrels—always in a hurry, high-strung, panicked like my adolescent self. Tree dwellers, as I was in childhood and even earlier, millions of years ago, when our species was cut off from the main genetic branch and cast onto the savannah to fend for ourselves. How desperate might we have been then to feed, to reproduce, to move, leaving our footprints in the newly settled ash of volcanoes? I'd read about them somewhere, those prehistoric footprints. They were uncovered in central Africa, three figures moving in a straight line—the Laetoli apeman and, presumably, his mate and child. At one point, the prints reveal that the apeman paused and turned himself to the west. I wondered what he saw—Food? A rival male? A mirage of trees? *Was he desperate?* Or was he just amazed at a world once again changing, transformed by forces beyond his understanding, the thick volcanic air pulling across his future like the skin of a snake? Within that pause, he might have felt a twinge, an inward turn toward his mate, his child, the source so deep it was beyond his memory, beyond the place where memory matters. In that place, there are no generations or species or nations, no blessings, no reasons to consider. In that place there is only the one reason: Life.

Then again, the ladder in my dream might represent the actual ladder in my garage, the one I should haul out and use to reach the gutters, desperate for cleaning. I can see from my window that they're clogged with leaves, which may also explain the tree image in my dream. I've been putting off cleaning them until, perhaps, I have a teenage son or daughter to do it for me. I look over and see that my neighbor has the same problem with his gutters. I haven't talked to Todd in a while. The last time I saw him he was standing in his still unterraced yard, dressed in a Green Bay Packers jersey, swinging at dandelions with a nine iron. Winter is almost here and I wonder what he's been doing to prepare? Despite my lingering suspicions, I'm half inclined to call him, to offer to help with his gutters. Maybe he'll offer to help me as well. Maybe, in the coming years of this generation, as we and our houses grow older, he and I are going to need each other more than we think, learning to exchange one of the few blessings we may have in us to give: goodwill.

In the meantime, the squirrels already cross the boundary between us, running from his yard to mine and back. I have no idea if what Todd said about them is true. At the moment, I see both black squirrels and red, but neither seems interested in hurting the other. They just seem busy. Between the oaks in Todd's yard and the walnuts in mine, they have a lot of work to do. I can hear them now, the walnuts, thudding against the ground. One after another, as if there will always be plenty, as if none of it matters.

WHY GEESE DON'T
WINTER IN PARADISE

"Where do the snow geese winter?" my student asked. We were standing on the edge of the lake, watching a few of the white birds glide on the black water, small, brilliant clouds against a receding storm.

"Oh," I said, startled from the sleep of other thoughts, "somewhere in the tropics, I believe. South America."

This was wrong, and another student shyly corrected me, repeating what I'd told them in class, that these geese migrate from the western coast of Hudson Bay to the Gulf Coast of Texas. That's where they spend the winter, in Texas. I quickly agreed with her and, feeling the blood burn in my cheeks, stepped back from the shore.

I was embarrassed, but not for the reasons one might think. These were graduate students in my environmental literature course, and I had brought them to western Iowa's DeSoto National Wildlife Refuge, near the town where I live, to witness one of the truly remarkable migratory events in the region: the fall stopover of snow geese along the Missouri River. The few birds we'd seen were beautiful, but disappointing—I had told them to expect flocks of thousands, which are common that

215

time of year. I had told them other things about the species as well, its coloration patterns, its mating and nesting habits, and yes, its migratory routes. I had done my research. Yet, when asked a simple question about the birds, I had without pause given an inaccurate, seemingly random response.

This factual inaccuracy is why I should have been embarrassed. Instead, the reason was that I'd been caught inside an intensely personal moment. When the student asked his question, I had been remembering the last time I'd seen geese, several weeks earlier, just minutes after my grandfather died. I'd been thinking of my grandfather and the geese, together. I'd been floating inside that surprising connection, confronted—as I sometimes am in nature, despite the facts—with forgotten desires, with questions asked and almost answered, with promises, as yet unfulfilled, of some kind of resolution. I had, in short, been caught inside a dream.

Here's how it went: My mother calls me on a Saturday morning in late September to say that Grandpa Andy, her father, will probably not live out the afternoon. She asks if I want to join them at the nursing home in Fort Dodge. At first, I hesitate: He's unconscious, and even if he weren't, he's had trouble recognizing me lately. Then I feel the empty space his death will carve inside my life, my body, and I have to be near him. Steph and I rush to the car and make the trip in record time. We're not too late; he's still alive. Most of our family is gathered around the bed: Grandma Kathryn, my parents, my sisters. Behind us, slumped in her wheelchair, is Grandpa's elder sister, Esther. Her hands are folded over her waist, covering the chickadee print on her oversized pink sweatshirt. She and

Grandpa have been roommates at the home for several years, but recently they've had trouble getting along. Esther has complained about his hallucinations: They're crazy, she says, though she herself has begun to tell crazy stories. In this moment, though, Esther is an afterthought; Grandpa, his dying, is at the center of our concern. His eyes are partially open, crescents of white; his breath is shallow, irregular. I hear the death rattle. Someone says it's a blessing, that he wouldn't want to live this way anymore. We take turns holding his hand, the good hand, the one that keeps reaching out into space, grasping. Someone says he needs us.

We have been with him for four hours straight when my father suggests we leave to get dinner. We will be quick, nothing will change, nothing has changed. We wheel Esther up to the side of Grandpa's bed—she doesn't seem to understand what's happening—place his flailing hand in hers, and leave. At the restaurant, not twenty minutes later, we get the call that he has died. Grandma Kathryn cries, says she should have stayed with him. Carrie Anne tries to comfort her, saying that when she worked at a nursing home this was how many of the residents passed away, often during the few minutes it took for a loved one to step outside to get a drink of water. It was as if they chose to die that way, on their own terms. That would be just like Grandpa, I tell her. Doesn't the caption beneath his 1928 yearbook photo read, *Muse not that I thus suddenly proceed; For what I will, I will, and there an end*? Yes, Grandma whimpers as I help her into the car, that's how he was.

I close her door, and when I turn around, I see them. The geese.

I didn't think much about them at the time, a half dozen Canadas flying low over the parking lot. Migrating geese are a common sight that time of year. And I certainly made no symbolic connection between them and my grandfather—nature had never been part of the vocabulary of our relationship. With him, there had been no campouts, no gardening, no fishing or hunting trips. Beyond the sunny, well-groomed slip of a golf course, he hadn't seemed to care for the outdoors. This fact, like the geese over the parking lot, had never seemed unusual. Fort Dodge, the hometown we shared, was small, industrial, a place that neither contained nor stood witness to what one might call the undeniable poetry of the wild. I'd also considered that as a young man my grandfather might have come to associate nature with the often brutal labor that the Depression had forced on him: digging ditches, shoveling coal, spreading creosote. That he might have been glad to achieve the cramped, but interior, walls of a manager's office—one of the places I most associated with him. Others included the small white living room where he taught my sisters and me how to shuffle cards; the looming cavern of the Gas and Electric service garage, where he let me blast the truck horns; and the cryptic facade of the Masonic Temple, where, at Christmas, he passed out toys to children in need. Grandpa's generosity and kindness and fallibility were, in my memory, mostly played out within these artificial structures of home. I had believed, as a boy, that he was indelibly anchored to them and, because I loved him desperately, to us.

I was surprised and hurt, as a child, when he and Grandma moved to Green Valley, Arizona. In retrospect, though, I can see the signs of the migrant spirit. His parents were Swedish immigrants, and as a boy, he liked to hop freight trains to Sioux City or Omaha to caddy at golf tournaments. Later, as a young man, he liked to drive fast, colorful cars along country roads. He liked to dance; he liked to drink, which can be another kind of absence. Grandpa was always restless, I now recall, fidgeting in his seat, soon up to play with us or wrestle. His body itself became a landscape on which we traveled, riding his shoulders, climbing his legs as if they were trees. So, it shouldn't have been a surprise that after the immigrant parents were dead, the daughter grown, the job finished, he had decided to leave Fort Dodge. Especially for Arizona, where it is always warm, where he would be free to walk the golf courses and mountain trails all year, free to dream of another kind of life. Perhaps one spent outdoors.

For a few months after they moved, that's exactly what he did. Then, in the middle of a patio bridge game—the Sonora moon was full that evening, my grandmother told me, and the quail were singing—there was a numbness in his arm, a darkness, a slumping beneath the table. In the years following the stroke, he would learn to move again, to sit, to walk, but not very far, only the couple of blocks to the pool and back. Mostly, he would sit in his chair in the sunroom and watch the television or the evening light as it swooned across the Santa Ritas, even more imprisoned by place than he'd been in Fort Dodge. *Imprisoned* was the word I often used—it's how I assumed I would've felt, if I were him—but as with the snow geese, as with many of the assumptions I make about life beyond me, I was wrong. Grandpa was not imprisoned; he was just beginning to move.

On the deck at the DeSoto visitor center, the students and I passed around a pair of binoculars to look for bald eagles. During my turn, I scanned the tree line and spotted a few white heads flaring like votives against the dun branches. I passed the binoculars to the student next to me, and continued searching the skies. I caught the wobbly sliver of a turkey vulture. We are made of dust, the minister had said at my grandfather's funeral, and to it we return. *But what of the air?* I thought. More than the earth, the air caresses and enfolds our bodies; it penetrates, migrating through the lungs, becoming rivers of blood, the tributaries of flesh and spirit. The air never truly leaves us, until the end. Yet, when asked, I can barely find the words to describe it: cold and warm, dry and humid, stable and unstable. Sometimes, during the spring storms—the floods, the tornadoes—I've heard it called "crazy." But what I was reminded of in the visitor center is that whatever else it might be called, the air here is also full. Of wind, of cloud, of birds—all of it moving or migrating. Right then, the students and I were concerned with birds, and though there weren't as many snow geese as we'd hoped, there were the bald eagles and the vulture. The eagles were moving from Alaska to Mexico, while the turkey vulture might soar all the way to the tropical heart of South America. Those are the kind of grand distances I liked to imagine when thinking of migration, journeys worthy of recognition, even celebration, such as the one I'd heard about in Hinckley, Ohio, where each spring residents welcome the vultures back from their odyssey. Not quite the swallows of San Juan Capistrano, but remarkable for its singularity, here where the migrations are so prominent and the celebrations of them so rare.

Whether he noticed it or not (and I'd always assumed he did not), my grandfather was raised within this full, migratory air. Any wonder that when his body became confined to chairs, his mind took flight? It was a family friend who first noticed. During her visit to Green Valley, she told Grandma that she'd been sitting with him in the living room watching *Guiding Light* when he picked up the phone, dialed Houston information, and asked if there was a listing under his name, Harold T. Anderson. A few minutes later he was on the line with a complete stranger, Harold C. Anderson, asking him if he was sure he owned the house he lived in.

"But Andy was a perfect gentleman," the friend said. "You'd never have known he was, well, *funny.*"

The doctor eventually diagnosed arteriosclerosis, describing how the vessels in my grandfather's brain were hardening, restricting the flow of blood. He warned that the hallucinations and amnesia would probably get worse. When I first heard this, I felt a rush of panic. I was in grad school, and though Grandpa had lived in Arizona for fifteen years, though I had grown up without him, I believed he still had a significant role to play in my life. I was, for the first time, awakening to the necessary complexities of commitment—to a long-term relationship with Steph, to an impoverished career as an academic, to what seemed to me an increasingly solidified, unimpressive future. More than anything, I wanted to leave that future behind and set out for the unknown territory, the unknown self. I had a feeling that, of all the people in my life, Grandpa might understand this desire to fly, might even grant me the permission, the courage, to embrace it. After all these years, the stories of our lives might still entwine. But not if he forgot me.

A short time later, after Steph and I decided to indefinitely postpone marriage, I took a cross-country car trip, then booked a flight from San Francisco to Arizona. Grandma picked me up at the airport and, during the car ride to Green Valley, told me that the hallucinations had gotten worse. She pleaded with me to corroborate that he had never gone to Texas, never gone anywhere since the stroke. Together, she thought we might be able to bring him back to reality. I had resisted her savior role in the past, but this time I nodded and prepared myself to be strong, to find gentle ways to correct him. For Grandma's sake and my own.

When I arrived, Grandpa was watching television in the sunroom, zipped tight inside his navy blue sweat suit. His face had aged since I last saw it two years ago, a bit more gaunt, but it still possessed a handsome, stubborn intelligence that led me to hope things weren't as bad as I'd been told. When he saw me, he straightened his back and smiled.

"Sit down," he said, after Grandma left to cook dinner. "I have something to ask you." He reached out his good hand and touched my arm. "As you know, Grandma kicked you and me out of the house a couple years ago and into the desert. She told us not to come back until you grew up and I could take care of myself. She was sick of us, and who can blame her, the way we behave. So we decided to hitchhike to Las Vegas, and along the way this skinny fellow, Jack Anderson, pulled over and said he was from ABC News and was looking for a good story. He'd heard we were going on an adventure and wanted to film us. I told him, 'Sure, but you better keep up—we're not slowing down for the likes of you.'"

And so my grandfather and I took off, first to Vegas, where he whipped Mohammed Ali in a street fight and earned us an invitation to join the Olympic boxing team. When President Carter boycotted the games, we decided to go to Moscow anyway and returned home laden with gold medals (we'd filled in for the American track team, as well). After the ticker tape parades subsided, we played a few legendary years of football at Johns Hopkins University. Forgoing our pro careers, we moved to Texas to enroll in graduate school at the University of Houston, where I majored in English and he majored in "Acupuncture," studying with the world famous Dr. Chang.

"Now, this is where you come in," he said. "I need to get back to my house in Houston to get my needles. If I can get my needles, I can heal myself and make some damn money. Have you brought the car?"

"No. I'm sorry."

"That's too bad," he said, and fell silent. We watched television.

The next morning, I overheard Grandma scolding him in the sunroom.

"Andy," she said, "John was only ten years old when all of this supposedly happened. He couldn't have gone on some crazy trip to Russia or wherever. John knows that since your stroke you aren't able to travel. John knows that, but he doesn't say anything because he doesn't want to hurt your feelings—Can't you see that? You just have to come back to reality, Andy; we all love you too much."

I sat in the bedroom, listening to Grandma slam pots in the kitchen sink while Grandpa deliberately munched his raisin bran. I felt guilty for betraying her, for not doing more to anchor Grandpa in place and time, but there was something about his story that had forged its own allegiance. In a week, I would be heading home to Iowa, to the same decisions I'd left behind. I didn't want to go back. I wanted, in one form or another, to keep moving. Forever.

"So where did we go after Houston?" I asked, quietly, when I joined him for breakfast. He grinned.

"She thinks I'm dreaming all of this up," he said, shaking his spoon at the kitchen, scattering droplets of milk. "She says I don't know the difference between dream and reality, but I know the difference. I'll tell you about a dream—just the other night I'm golfing on this beautiful course in Florida. I need to take a leak, so I walk over to the bushes and unzip. I woke up and found myself standing between the beds, pissing all over my meds on the table. Now that, goddammit, is a *dream!*"

Inside the visitor center, the students and I studied an aerial photo of DeSoto Bend prior to 1960, when the U.S. Army Corps of Engineers straightened or, as the tour booklet said, "stabilized" the Missouri River channel. The photo reminded me of something my father-in-law, a physicist, once said about fractal geometry, how the most beautiful images occur inside the mathematical border between stability and instability. He showed me some of those images on his computer, brilliant blossoms of color which, though unpredictable, conjured familiar associations: trees, mountains, lightning. In the aerial photo, the unstable Missouri River looked like a fractal image, its boundaries irregular and unclear, but more interesting than the nearly Euclidian line it had become. Back then the river, like the air, was migratory, meandering one way then another, blurring the border between states, creating sandbars and shallow wetlands and oxbow lakes. In those borderlands between stability and instability, the beautiful things did indeed occur: the blossoming of wetland flowers and grasses, the gathering of wildlife, the sustenance of innumerable birds.

Some version of that beauty remained inside the visitor center, displayed in photographs or glassed-in dioramas. There was a grouping of snow and blue geese in an autumn cornfield, a pair of bald eagles, a sand hill crane. There was a bobcat leaping at a bobwhite, two sun-bleached beavers, a river otter, and a lonely mink. A pallid sturgeon—one of the Missouri's ancient and now threatened species—hung by wire from the ceiling. These creatures were stuffed and immobile, yet they still had the power to evoke a sense of concern and responsibility that led, as intended, straight to the donation box. But when I opened my wallet and discovered I had only a ten, I reconsidered: *Too much? Too little?* In the mornings, while munching my own spoonfuls of raisin bran, I'd sometimes caught a back-page article on the sorry state of the Missouri, on the hundreds of thousands of habitat acres lost since channelization, on the continuing disappearance of its native wildlife. Other articles had informed me that, in the interests of preserving that wildlife, the Army Corps of Engineers was considering restoring some of the original flow of the river, allowing controlled floods in the spring and lower levels in the summer. If this plan were ever approved, it might be evidence that this dammed, poisoned place continues to dream. Continues to shape and absorb the dreams of others. That's another kind of power, I thought, and dropped the ten in the box.

One of my last visits to Green Valley, before my grandfather returned to Fort Dodge to die, occurred just after my wedding. Following the ceremony, Steph and I spent a few memorable days in the Sawtooth wilderness of Idaho and then caught a flight to Tucson. It was my idea. On the altar of the church, during the ceremony, we had placed a single red rose in memory of deceased relatives. These included my paternal grandfather, Roy, who had been allowed the dignity to die of a heart attack while I was still in high school, long before he might have lost his mind or our idolization. Grandpa Andy was alive, yet he was less of a presence at my wedding than the dead. I wanted him to be part of the celebration, part of its real memory.

When we arrived, Grandpa was still in his chair in the sunroom, watching television. I introduced Steph. He took her hand and softly kissed it.

"Hello, beautiful," he said. "Did I ever tell you about the time John wrestled a grizzly bear in Idaho?"

The next morning, Grandma asked if I wouldn't mind putting some of that wasted medical training to work and help Grandpa with his shower. She wanted to show Steph her roses, she said, but I knew that what she really wanted was a break. So I helped him to the bathroom and undressed him as he sat on the toilet. When I removed his shirt, I noticed how the muscles in his left arm had almost vanished, how the cavities near his shoulders—the shoulders I'd once climbed—had eroded, as deep as canyons. They seemed to measure how much we'd truly missed of each other, our bodies growing older. When Grandpa began, once again, to talk about our Idaho adventures, I became impatient. I hadn't come all the way to Arizona for this. This time, I had come for something real.

"Grandpa, I was only in seventh grade," I interrupted. "There's no way I could've put a full nelson on a grizzly, let alone snapped its neck. I was a puny kid, anyway—*Remember?*"

"Well, you grew up in a hurry that year."

"I didn't grow up that fast."

In the shower chair, he began the story once again. I tried to interrupt, but he took hold of my wrist and squeezed it surprisingly hard.

"Now, hang on," he said. "Just *listen,* for once!"

He explained that, in fact, he had lived two lives. In the first, he'd lived in Fort Dodge, Iowa, and worked for the gas and electric company and moved to Arizona and had a stroke. The adventures he was talking about occurred during his second life, his "second chance" as he called it. As he told me this, I washed his rigid, useless left arm, his wilted torso, and concluded, finally, that the opportunity for any kind of meaningful connection with this man had vanished a long time ago. Beyond his physical presence, he wasn't capable of giving me much. I, on the other hand, could at least give him my silent attention.

"You think you were puny, John," he continued, "but what I keep trying to tell you is you *weren't.* You were huge, seven foot umpteen inches. Of course, I was eight foot myself, but believe me, you were something to behold."

He'd told me this before, but now I was listening in a different way, my hands on his naked body, an intimacy we had never known. Minutes earlier, I'd felt his nearly dead weight against my shoulder as I helped him into the shower. He was a large, heavy man, but I knew from photos that he'd been a small boy. I'd been small, too, an experience that had cost me a lot of adolescent anguish. Had my grandfather noticed? Is that what his

dreams were about? Not just the athletic disappointments of being short (Olympic boxing?), but also my failed effort to become a medical doctor (Johns Hopkins?), my drift toward
writing and literature (English at Houston?), my fear of com-
mitting to Steph (the bear in Idaho?), and, of course, my desire
to leave home. It wasn't just me; I recalled others in my family
who had visited Grandpa in the desert and returned with crazy
but personal stories: Carrie Anne, who had fought her way
through school and a disastrous relationship, was a general in
the army; Susan, the animal lover, owned a lucrative farm;
Allyson, the youngest, had climbed to the top of Kilimanjaro.
Mom had become thin and healthy and rich thanks to Grandpa's acupuncture sessions. The truth of these stories, though
factually inaccurate, had finally reached me. All along—was it
the letters, the phone calls, the terrain of our faces?—he had
understood the insides of our desires, had cared, had wanted to
help. He had been far away, and yet he had known me. Still
knew me.

"You wrote it all down," he said. "It's going to be your first
book. You're going to make millions on the movie."

"I hope so," I said, rinsing the soap from his body. "And
who'll play our parts?"

"Ah, hell," he said. "We'll play ourselves."

I wonder if, while growing up in Iowa, my grandfather ever
came to know the Missouri River, its earlier, restless self. He
would have crossed over it in those rickety boxcars when he was
a boy. I wonder if, many years later, he looked at the river from
the window of the jet that finally brought him home, from Ari-

zona to Fort Dodge, after he broke his hip and Grandma could no longer care for him. If he did, he would have seen a much different river, the one I was now standing beside, straight and fast and cold. My students and I were walking along the levee, reading how the Corps built it in 1960 to create DeSoto's oxbow lake, the lake the geese come to every year. Although the brochure didn't say so, it was obvious that the new river was no longer an option for the geese: If they landed there, they would be swept away like squawking kids on a waterslide. The lake is all they have. "Maybe," a student thought aloud, "if the Corps does change the flow, there'll be more places for the geese and other birds to rest along the river." We nodded and I tried to imagine that beautiful, immense return, but inevitably I was drawn back to the river as it is. Unable to move, it digs down into itself, its banks standing sliced and exposed like butcher's meat. The Missouri has been declared one of the most endangered rivers in the nation, which is another way of saying it is in the act of forgetting itself. This amnesia—that we allow it to happen—is one of the reasons why I'm sometimes ashamed to say I live here, why I'm still tempted to leave. By moving, the fantasy goes, I might avoid witnessing the destruction of the places I care about, the places that created me. I might even find a place where people live a different, more enlightened story on the land. At the very least, I might avoid moments like the one on the levee when, against our silence, the river seemed to amplify the collective judgment: You do not deserve what little wildness you enjoy.

But what other story is possible? No matter where we live, our touch seems to incur shame and forgetfulness, whether it be the natural course of a river or the aging lives of the people we love. That's what those "care facilities" are all about, no matter how clean or well run. As soon as Grandpa was wheeled into that cramped room, he began truly to forget. Within a few years, he had lost all of his first life and most of his second. They were replaced by more immediate, but less inspiring, stories about residents hitting him in the head with chairs. For a long time, he hung onto the house in Houston, but eventually even that dissolved, and I didn't miss it. His stories became, for me, less about freedom and more about the pitiful restrictions of his life. I'd forgotten what I'd supposedly learned while bathing Grandpa in Arizona: to listen carefully to even the most restricted spirit. Even when, during one of my infrequent visits to his room in Fort Dodge, he said, "It's good to be home," I did not hear what he was trying to tell me. Instead, I focused on the limited view out his window, the screams of the insane, the pungent odor of disinfectant and urine, the imminence of death. Despite all those years wishing my grandfather had stayed in Iowa, I had, in truth, always imagined him dying in Arizona, his eyes on the mountains, the still lucid desert, his spirit on the move. This was not where his journey—or mine— was supposed to end, in the very place where it had begun. A migration, after all.

"How is it you thought the geese wintered in a tropical paradise?" another student asked as we walked back to the visitor center. She was smiling, teasing—the autumn wind was cold. I shrugged: "You know, ancient Europeans thought geese wintered on the moon—at least I'm closer than they were."

But what I really wanted to say was "That's how far I'd go, if I were a bird. If I were a man's dream."

When we returned to Grandpa's room, it seemed cavernous without the sounds of his dying. We gathered around his bed and laid our hands on his body, still warm. Mom picked up his left hand, the bad one, no longer twisted and cramped. For the first time since the stroke, she was able to place her fingers inside his and draw them to her face. "Look at that," she said. "This is my father."

We were each given a few minutes alone with his body. During my turn, I circled the bed, looking for the rise of his chest, the twitch of his mouth and arms, the thump of his heart through the pajamas, realizing how active even his dying body had been. Inside that stillness, I had the distinct sense, as people often do, that the person I loved was somewhere else. I knelt beside him and prayed that wherever that place was, it was far away from Iowa: Houston, the Sonora—Paradise. Far away, just as I thought he'd always hoped to be.

"Did you hear the geese?"

I turned and saw Esther—she'd been there the entire time, unnoticed in her bed at the far end of the room, covers pulled up to her chin.

"Pardon?" I said.

"Did you hear the geese?"

I told her I'd seen some geese above the restaurant parking lot.

"I heard them," she said, her voice almost too low to understand. "Harold always used to call me, in the fall, when he saw the first geese flying south. He'd say, 'Sister, did you see the geese?' Just yesterday, he said that to me. He saw them out his window."

Muse not that I thus suddenly proceed. Yet, that's exactly what I do back at the DeSoto parking lot. My students have already left without seeing the big flocks. I'm ready to go myself, but have paused to admire the fiery scallops of the disappearing sun. This is the time of day when my grandfather died, holding hands with his sister. He chose, if there be such a choice, to end with her, in that place, in this season. He had noticed the geese every year, had loved in his own way the cycles of the land. It held, still holds, the restless spirit that defined him. Even the sky—I can already see a few stars. Soon, if the evening is clear, I'll be able to spot Orion and my favorite, Vega, a blue-white star much bigger than our own. Vega used to be the North Star, and it will be so again in another twelve thousand years. It will guide, once more, the transient and the lost, including this sun, this planet, which are moving toward it. We won't arrive for hundreds of millions of years, but still, when I look at Vega through my binoculars, I think I see, among all the stars, a special brilliance. The fire that lights the end of our story.

So, it will be dark soon, but not yet. The brilliance of the day seems, in fact, to be growing, covering the sky with gold. Near the zenith, there is a smudge of shadow. It becomes larger, noisier, more irregular. And then they are above me, the snow geese, thousands of them returning from the fields, blotting out the sky just as I have always imagined and hoped they would. I'm sorry my students aren't here to see it—Will they believe me when I tell them?—but I'm here, and I am thankful. Thankful, despite everything, to be home. The way he was. I wonder if that would surprise him, to know that in my memory he is forever linked with these birds, that they have become for me his life's articulation. That wherever else we might travel together, he is also here, watching the geese return to the Missouri River. I stare into their loud, shimmering depths and lose my bearings—Who is moving, who is still? Who is alive, dead? Can anything be truly lost or forgotten? I look for the answers. They fly on, blurring, as they always have, the border between fact and desire. Rivers upon rivers, flowing forever.

Now that—I can almost hear him say—is a dream.

MOON KITTY

I'm sitting in the lawn chair, watching our ten-month-old son, Ben, and our four-year-old cat, Tigger, explore the backyard. Inside, Steph is enjoying a much deserved rest. Tigger has been prowling the brushy borders of the woods, and Ben, naked, has been crawling behind him. Tigger has paused near the daylilies—perhaps he's spotted something dead or unwisely moving, unaware of the great white whale, as we call him, the giant feline clown with the liver spots and scary pink nipples. Tigger is a twenty-five-pounder, the biggest cat most people have ever seen. He is wiggling his generous caboose, ready to pounce, when Ben crawls up and nudges into him. Startled, the cat swerves and bops Ben on the face—*thwap, thwap, thwap.* I consider intervening, but Ben only giggles. He has clearly mistaken the face-bopping for something else, maybe love. He parks himself next to the cat and, together, they stare into the lilies— whatever was there, or between them, is gone. There is only the dappled shade, the newly warm breeze calling out the insects, the birds. The antiphonal prelude to summer.

This excursion is a serious crime and there will be consequences. Or so we've been told. Despite being neutered, Tigger has been spraying the couch, which the vet claims is because we let him outside too much. When the spraying first occurred, ten months ago, the vet claimed it was because of the new baby. Tigger was jealous, she explained, territorial, as males, even neutered, can be. I could relate. Steph had introduced a new member to the pride, a furless creature of surprising power; without fang or claw or control of limb, it managed to procure the choicest bits from the hunt, the sweetest morsels of affection. Tigger's response, at first, was to hide in the basement for days. Then, one morning, Steph sat down on the couch to nurse and asked, "Do you smell something?" That smell soon spread to everything associated with the baby: stuffed animals, bouncy chair, diaper cloths, breast pump. We read books and consulted the vet and tried various strategies, but all fell predictably short of what Tigger clearly desired: that the farting, kvetching thing be gotten rid of. When it became clear that that wasn't going to happen, he turned on Steph and me, spraying my shoes, Steph's scrapbooks, my student papers, our library books, and any jacket draped too casually over the kitchen chair.

We kicked him outdoors for the rest of the summer and fall. When winter approached, we let him back inside. This, apparently, was our big mistake. If we'd kept him inside the entire time, the vet lectured, he would've eventually gotten used to the baby and perhaps stopped spraying, but not now. You cannot simply let a housecat outdoors and then bring him back in and expect him to act civilized. Something happens to them out there; something awakens that will no longer sleep. But this is Iowa, we replied. It gets cold in the winter. Predators are hungrier, meaner than usual. To them, Tigger would appear as large and flashy as roadhouse neon. He'd be eaten alive.

So we kept him inside and the winter was misery. At Christmas he targeted the things most intimate to us, most sentimental—the tenderly wrapped presents, the antique Santa doll, the stockings. The lower branches of our tree, though artificial, appeared to be wilting. The smell only got worse after the holidays, the windows shut tight, the spirit dissipated. How does one describe it? The bouquet, like that of a bad wine, conveyed disarming contradictions: fruity yet metallic, sweet yet cynical, naïve yet barbaric. As a rhetorical strategy, it was irresistible, a signifier that remained intimately entwined with the signified. It reeked of warning, of fury—the very dregs of despair. As a territorial marker, it strongly discouraged unnecessary loitering: *Just passing through, thanks.* Watching TV on the couch became an act of endurance. Eating there was out of the question. All winter, during our most precious times with the baby—the cuddling, the playing, the Madonna-like moments of nursing—we were reminded, through the stench, of Tigger's displeasure, his jealous love.

The first warm day of the year—the first above freezing, anyway—we kicked him outside again. The enzymatic cleaners finally took hold and the house has become livable, if only barely. The stench is still strong enough to drive us outdoors in nice weather, like today, and I'm grateful for it. I think Ben is grateful, too, but for reasons more closely allied with Tigger's. Out here, he and the cat are free—free to roam, to pee where they please. Out here, there is no tyranny of the litter box, no diaper enslavement. Since coming outside they have, in fact, both peed in the grass. I wonder what Ben is learning from the cat—what is being awakened—and if I should be worried. Lately, Ben has been bopping people in the face with his tiny fist and the shadow of blame has fallen on Tigger who, as witnessed earlier, is a known face-bopper. This is a serious public issue—Ben broke my glasses at a restaurant on Valentine's Day, and on Easter Sunday, he gave Grandma a fat lip. It has become yet another reason to separate him from the cat, perhaps permanently. I admit we've considered this. But right now we're outdoors and it's spring. The winter has been survived; the long, fragrant hibernation is over. It's time to wake up, to fresh air, to life. It's time to think of other things.

Like that I'm a father—I have yet to fully awaken to this reality. It wasn't that long ago that we found out Steph was pregnant (by natural means, after all), and began converting the guest room. Like most baby rooms before actual occupation, it was neat and color-coordinated and brilliantly creative, like the child with whom we'd surely be blessed. Before the baby shower, my mother had asked what theme we'd chosen. Steph scoffed at this request, this obsession with thematic baby rooms, dismissing it as a "Midwestern thing." Themes only cause trouble, she said, referring indirectly (and thus very Midwesternly, I thought) to my sisters. When Susan got pregnant a few years ago, she announced that the theme for her baby shower would be Winnie-the-Pooh. A couple of weeks later, Carrie Anne got pregnant and announced that she, too, would hold a Pooh-themed baby shower. Susan was furious—another example of Big Sister stealing the show. After intense negotiation, it was agreed that Carrie Anne's theme would be Disney Pooh, while Susan's would be Classic Pooh. This hair's-breadth zoological distinction saved, at least temporarily, the Hundred Acre Wood known as my sisters' love for one another.

Steph viciously mocked the "Pooh Wars," but then, one Sunday, she was perusing newspaper ads and discovered a child's bedspread sporting faux quilt squares with stitched images of bears and cabins and pine trees. "This reminds me of home," she said. Within days the baby's room sprouted forests and mountain ranges and moose, all of them waiting, here in the grasslands, to impress themselves on our child's imagination and memory, as they have his mother's.

I viciously mocked Steph (in private) but then, a month later, found myself standing on a ladder sticking glow-in-the-dark stars to the ceiling of the baby's room. I told Steph it was my contribution to the Idaho theme, but in truth, it was a different theme altogether, one I didn't completely understand. I'd bought the stars shortly after the ultrasound. We'd decided before our appointment that, when it came to gender, we didn't want to know, that we would let it be the baby's secret, his or her special surprise. This conviction made us feel superior to other expecting couples, countercultural, already putting the child's self-esteem before our own. Once we were inside the clinic, however, it didn't take long to digress. When the nurse squirted goo on Steph's belly, I was immediately transported to kindergarten, spreading goo on my misshapen and condemned papier-mâché piñata, getting ready to excuse myself to go vomit. This baby will learn about papier-mâché piñatas, I thought, and it will be troubling. There is the deformed image itself, of course, but also all that it implies about the world we live in, the future—strangers and friends beating your beloved, beautiful creation with sticks until the guts spill out and then eating it alive. And you, standing on the sidelines, helpless, wanting to save that creation—*Why can't they see how beautiful it is?*—but succeeding only in growing old.

That's how the thinking goes at the ultrasound until, on the screen, a hand emerges from the inky darkness. Then arms and feet and a round, healthy skull, and once again I'm a child, this time caressing my Magic 8-Ball and making wishes and receiving only happy affirmations: *Outlook Good. Without a Doubt. It Is Certain. It Is Decidedly So. Yes. Yes Definitely.* The angle moves wide, taking in the entire body of our child, a glorious, iridescent landscape, alive and stretching . . . and then something unexpected rises from the blackness, just above the thigh, gleaming like a moonlit dagger.

A boy. The nurse didn't confirm it, but that was my assumption and I was surprised by how strongly it affected me. I retreated to the basement for days, dusting off my Matchbox car collection, my Star Wars figures, my comic books. An only boy, I'd finally have someone to play with. A little later, in the checkout lane at the drugstore, I spotted the bag of glow-in-the-dark stars hanging alongside other plastic nonsense in a distant aisle. I interrupted the clerk and retreated all the way back through the line, because, for some reason, I'd die without those stars.

Tigger watched that evening as I stuck the stars to the ceiling, swishing his tail. He was curious, I suppose, and a little anxious. We'd completely rearranged what used to be his exclusive space, perhaps already provoking an ominous tingle in his loins. And now this. I offered him no assurances, because I had none to give—I was curious about the stars myself and a little anxious. I'd had stars on my ceiling as a boy. I remembered my mom sticking them there when she was pregnant with James, and how close they seemed at the top of our bunk bed. Within reach, even. I remembered a moon, as well, but perhaps it was only the real moon, shining through the window. That's where the babies live, my mother once explained, lying next to me, her pregnant belly large and dark in my sight, like a hill, like a landscape. They live on the moon, waiting to be called down to earth. And then I'm afraid, because the ladder is tall and unstable, and to be born is no small thing. It can go wrong, babies can be lost, as James was, and I know how easily hope can then become a kind of curse, following you through the years to a moment like this, making it difficult to surrender.

I couldn't finish. I stepped down the ladder and left Tigger alone in the room, staring at the strange and incomplete constellation.

In the backyard, Tigger and Ben are now crawling near a patch of Solomon's seal, a woodland flower I've come to appreciate. A member of the lily family, its botanical name is from the Greek for "many knees," while its common name refers to the circular scars on the stem believed to resemble the ancient seal of King Solomon. These scars mark the previous year's growth, a kind of body memory, revealing its age. It has many healing properties. Pioneers used it for hemorrhoids, arthritis, poison ivy, and to diminish freckles. Tribal cultures used it for kidney trouble and back pains, storing it in bags made of bear paws to preserve its power. That was when bears could be found in this region, before the prairies and oak savannahs were almost completely destroyed. This has become another kind of theme, though not a chosen one, seeing what should be here but isn't. It's a theme

Steph might be justified in calling Midwestern, born as it is from a traumatic ecological loss never fully acknowledged or grieved. It's also annoying. A friend once called me a "prairie snob" for referring to the giant hackberries in our yard as "junk." He was right, I suppose. The hackberries, like the Solomon's seal and the young woods, shouldn't be dismissed any more than the prairie should be. Still, to let go of that deeper past, even for a moment, feels like another kind of surrender.

The boy and the cat, however, do not acknowledge such boundaries. They mark their own. Somewhere, near the daylilies, their pee smells are intermingling, rising to the breeze, an entirely new language expressing . . . *What?* Warning? Invitation? Forgiveness? The possibilities inspire me to get down on my own hands and knees—What will I discover?—and I immediately feel like a fool. I crawl to a discreet, overgrown corner of the yard, out of view of the neighbors. From there, I can see why our backyard is regarded as a crime. No chemicals or fertilizer, the grass competes to live here like all the rest: the creeping charlie, the phlox, the periwinkle, the poison ivy, the clover. The squirrels and moles, their tunnels snaking everywhere. The yard is ruined, we've been told, but that doesn't seem to be the case. It is colorful, the diverse greens flickering in the various kinds of shade from the various kinds of leaves: bur oak, linden, black walnut, and, yes, hackberry. The boy and the cat can crawl in that shade, on this ground, without worry. We have that, at least.

Across the way, Ben lets out a barbaric yawp and raises something soft and black in his hand, squeezing it between his fingers. He offers it to Tigger, who sniffs then slaps at his hand, knocking chunks of it free. I rise to my proper height and begin the concerned approach. Ben has a fistful of scat—*acky!* I take his wrist and shake it off his fingers, spattering it all over his body. I then turn the hose on him, blasting water on his hands, legs, and chest. There is some crying, but he will not let me comfort him in the lawn chair; he arches, trying to slide to the ground.

"Kitty!" he screams.

Tigger is sitting provocatively near the scat, glaring. Ben screams even louder and I give up—I am hopelessly outside this kinship between them. I let him down and follow him back to Tigger, back to the scat. We study it for a while. It is definitely not Tigger's—his piles are the size of a Shetland pony's. I recall seeing a red fox in the woods that winter; perhaps he's still around. Or maybe it belongs to a mountain lion. The lions have returned to western Iowa recently, to the Loess Hills where we live, making me a little more respectful of the dusk. Another instinct that, against all odds, has been awakened out here.

Of course, I'm no expert. The scat may have belonged to something more ordinary, like the neighbors' poodle, but after so many similar afternoons in the yard we—Ben, Steph, Tigger, and I—no longer think in terms of the ordinary. Ordinary is all about species hierarchies, chronological time, and the imprisonment of the senses. Ordinary is about distance. Our backyard is no longer ordinary, nor is the universe, which I've been noticing again. Especially the moon. We three watch it from the deck sometimes, late at night, while Steph gets another rest. When it is full, or near full like tonight, it seems unusually close, within reach, even. I am reminded that ancient Egyptians thought the sky was within reach, a kind of blanket held up by distant mountains. Ben takes a swipe at the moon; Tigger stares at it, in between stalking wood roaches. I stare at the moon as well, scratching my knees, which itch from crawling across the yard again that afternoon, penitent, no longer embarrassed. I am similarly humbled by this moment, the boy on my lap, the real stars, and then there is another memory, a psalm from child-hood: *Out of the mouths of babes, of infants at the breast, Thou has rebuked the mighty. . . . When I look up at Thy heavens, the work of Thy fingers, the moon and the stars set in their place by Thee, what is man that Thou shouldst care for him? Yet Thou has made him little less than a god. . . . Thou makest him master over all Thy creatures.*

"Kitty!" Ben screams, and perhaps it is this, the resistant child, the thought of the cat-fragrant winter to come, the wood roaches swarming beneath the deck, the psalm—we are definitely *not* gods—that makes me want to reestablish the boundaries.

"Moon," I say.

Ben swats the air—"Kitty!"—and I have to admit the moon does look a lot like Tigger. Which reminds me that those same ancient Egyptians worshipped cats as gods, and ancestors, and then the sad thoughts come, of the past giving way to the fu-ture, of all of us growing older, the natural order of things.

"Kitty!" he says.

"Moon," I say.

"Da-da!" he says and, at last, I surrender. I let it go, his voice, rising to meet the breeze, rising above the house, the clouds, beyond the moon and the stars, to join the eternal ether. Like all the other gestures that might be mistaken for love.

On Kalsow Prairie

(A Postlude)

It's almost dusk, though storm clouds obscure the exact position of the sun. I fear our time here will be too short. Ben and his younger brother, Spencer, now six and four years old, are heading southwest toward the fire-red blossoms of a butterfly milkweed, which, like all fire, attracts their kind. Steph is among the yellow coneflowers to the southeast. I'm on northern ground, literally, having just tripped over the swollen sod of prairie dropseed grass. I've decided I like the view from here— of the prairie, of my family. The ground is comfortably thatched and the low-lying hassock of dropseed, the very one that tripped me, has become the perfect place to prop my elbow. From here the mid-July grasses and flowers appear to tower over me, as do my children, my boys, which will be the case soon enough, in seasons to come.

When viewed from the road, Kalsow Prairie is nearly invisible against the taller corn of the surrounding fields. If not for the wooden sign, we might have missed it entirely. At 160 acres, Kalsow is what is commonly called a postage-stamp prairie, one of the last scattered vestiges of native tallgrass. I've always been intrigued by that metaphor, the idea that such places convey messages across space and time, which is true in a way. To those trying to restore prairie on cultivated or otherwise disturbed ground, these postage stamps are the guardians of heritage, the deliverers of seed and ancient knowledge. If they disappear, as many do, then it may not be possible for the land to go home again. "They are the last lingering scraps of the old time," John Madson wrote in *Where the Sky Began: Land of the Tallgrass Prairie*, "fragments of original wealth and beauty, cloaked with plants that you may never have seen before and may never see again." He was referring specifically to Kalsow Prairie, which is only a few miles west of Fort Dodge, though I don't remember hearing about it while living there. Like other treasures, I had no idea it was so close to home.

Not until Tillie, my great-grandmother, pointed the way.

We were in the midst of what is called a family weekend. On Saturday, we traveled to Des Moines for the annual Price family reunion, where I was able to catch up with many of my Iowa cousins, including Dave, who was there with his wife, Samantha, and their three children. The next day, my sisters and I took our families to visit the Grotto of the Redemption in West Bend, where our grandparents Roy and Mildred Price had often taken us as kids—a massive structure made of millions of shells, rocks, and other geological wonders intended to tell the story of humanity's redemption. It was started in 1912 by a local priest, Father Dobberstein, fulfilling a promise to Mother Mary, whose intercession had, he believed, saved him from death. We began our tour at the petrified Tree of Knowledge and made our way up the narrow path, two stories, past other grottoes depicting biblical scenes. The journey ended at the cross, beneath which is a marble reproduction of Michelangelo's *Pietá*, of Mary holding the body of Jesus. I remembered my grandfather Roy pointing out how Mary's face appeared younger than her son's. As a boy that had seemed as strange and haunting to me as the other story in that statue, a son dying before his mother.

We returned that evening to Fort Dodge, and as we piled into the house I was amazed again by what a large clan we'd become. Carrie Anne and her husband, Mark, have three girls, Abigail, Grace, and Anna. Allyson and her husband, Jason, have a two-year-old son, Owen. Susan was visiting from Montana, where she lives with husband Tim and nine-year-old Ian—the only sibling not residing in Iowa, though Steph is grateful for another familial link to the mountain West. Every bed and couch in our childhood home was occupied, as well as most of the floor space.

While looking for a place to sleep, I found myself standing in front of the simple wood-and-iron trunk, the one Tillie had brought with her from Sweden. It is an artifact from a branch of our family that is nearly gone: Tillie and John. Andy and Kathryn. Esther. There will be no Anderson family reunion, no more winter trips to Boone to sing Swedish songs. There is only what can be gathered around such artifacts, in memory and story. Tillie's trunk had been built for her by her older brother, Gus, his first project as a carpenter's apprentice in Sweden before emigrating to Minnesota. He gave it an arched lid, very difficult to craft, to discourage ship's porters from stacking other trunks on top of it. Tillie's ship was the *Campania*, of the Cunard Line, and the trunk still displays the stickers and stamps from its arrival at Ellis Island on November 1, 1902, when Tillie was twenty-eight. While examining those stickers, I noticed some faded writing on the front of the trunk: *Matilda Erlandson. Rossie Jova, North Amerika.*

Rossie, Iowa? Esther had never mentioned Rossie as her mother's initial destination, only her dismal arrival in Fort Dodge and the treacherous beau who had enticed her there. I retrieved an old state map my parents had from the thirties and located Rossie almost a hundred miles to the northwest, approaching the Minnesota border, not that far from where Tillie's brother had settled—Had that been her intention? Esther said Tillie had always been very close to Gus; he'd built the porch for their house on Haskell Street, where her father, John, rocked them and sang his *visas*, his story songs. Did that relationship, that kinship first bring her to this country, to Iowa? Had Tillie's suitor from Fort Dodge, hired to recruit for the factories, made his proposal in Sweden or in Rossie? I traced the rail line with my finger south from Rossie to a junction just west of Fort Dodge, labeled "Tara." Esther had said Tara was the place where her mother had first stepped off the train in Iowa, though I'd always assumed it was the name of some obscure township inside the borders of Fort Dodge, like old Swedetown and Bobtown. I couldn't find Tara labeled on any current state map, but while scanning the area I discovered yet another place I hadn't known I was seeking: Kalsow Prairie.

We were supposed to return home this morning—almost everyone else had left already—but I postponed our departure in order to take my family to Tara, then up to Kalsow. This was not a popular decision with the kids. They were tired and anxious to get home to feed the fish and let the cat out of the house—Tigger, never one to play favorites, had been spraying Spencer's bedspread. I was anxious about this myself, but as I explained to them on the way out of town, we were attending another family reunion of sorts.

"Will our cousins be there?" Ben asked.

"Will there be chips and pop?" Spencer added.

"I'm afraid not," I said.

Spencer responded by hitting the button on his puppy-shaped song maker, the one I've repeatedly asked him not to play while I'm driving. The cabin filled with a very loud, elec-trotwangy version of "The more we stick together, together, together . . ." It was a miracle, frankly, that in the midst of that noise we were able to concentrate long enough to find the gravel road leading to Tara, or what remains of it: basically an over-grown thicket hiding a few houses and buildings, most of them abandoned. The railroad junction was still there, still function-ing, and just to the east, nearly obscured by trees, was what looked to be the old station.

We walked along the tracks until we came to the dilapi-dated brick structure. It was no small chore keeping the boys from charging in and falling straight through the rotten floor. The only signs of past human occupancy were rusted barrels of grease, and a green metal chair parked on what remained of the loading platform.

"Who sits there?" Ben asked. "A ghost?" Ben has apparently inherited the Price fascination with the macabre.

"Maybe," I said. "Maybe your great-great-grandmother sat in it a hundred years ago, when she came here from Sweden."

This was a bit of a stretch—the chair didn't look to be from that time period and, as I would discover later, the original station had burned down. Even so, this was the spot where Tillie had likely waited to make the switch from the westbound train out of Chicago to the one bound north to Rossie. What would she have seen? The view from that green chair to the south was mostly of bean fields, but large swaths of unplowed land still bordered the tracks, filled with prairie plants: yellow coneflower, butterfly milkweed, purple prairie clover, wild indigo.

Spencer pointed out a goldfinch perched on a nearby cone-flower, and at least a dozen tiger swallowtail butterflies. Was there a larger version of this prairie here when Tillie arrived? It would have been early November, and depending on that autumn's weather, the prairie colors might have been dominated by dull grays and browns. Or, instead, the rich russet and wine and gold that the mature grasses often display, even in dormancy and death, their fluffy seed heads hovering and shifting above the ground like a mist. There may have been hawks in the air or cranes or a high flock of snow geese, a shimmering white cloud in the sea-blue November sky. For Tillie, there may have been something not entirely foreign in that view—a country running, as Willa Cather put it, moving, like her brother, like herself.

"I'm king of the sky!" Spencer proclaims, back at Kalsow. He has found a long switch of bluestem, lifts it into the air, sword-like, and brings it down hard onto the back of his elder brother. There is a yelp, a shove, then a lot of shouting. Steph is approaching them, so I can remain where the fathers of grassland species are most comfortable: on their side, in recline.

Still, it's not as if I'm free of concern. At the reunion, Dave told me he was speaking publicly again about youth violence, bringing to bear his current work as a counselor for at-risk kids, still trying to calm fears with information—fears we now share as fathers. As we talked, we were interrupted by the shouts of our children. Ben and Aaron, Dave's youngest son, along with a number of their cousins, had piled onto the net-enclosed trampoline for a jumping exercise that had quickly devolved into something resembling a WWF cage match—pushing, wrestling, flipping, body slams. We were about to put an end to it, but our fathers reminded us that it was just harmless fun, recalling how their own grandfather had forced them to wrestle their younger cousins in Missouri, while poking them with his cane. Good times.

I suppose they're right, what takes place on the trampoline is the least of our worries. I was reminded of this again, earlier today, while traveling through the small town of Manson, where I completed driver's education as a teenager. The thought of my boys as teenagers, tearing around the greater Omaha metropolitan area in a car, is truly frightening. In contrast, my classmates and I practiced parallel parking in the relatively empty downtown of Manson and casually cruised the rural highways, where oncoming traffic was limited to an occasional slow-going pickup. There were few opportunities for a fatal collision, which is probably why my parents had sent me there for training. Our instructor did his best to add some drama. He informed us that Manson is in the middle of what is called "storm alley," and that the nearby town of Pomeroy had once been completely destroyed by a tornado. He added that, millions of years ago, this whole area had been ground zero for a massive meteor strike.

"You hotshots may survive drivers' education," he'd said, "but that won't save you from the next killer tornado or asteroid."

We laughed then, but he may have been right. The asteroid Apophis, named for the Egyptian god of darkness and evil, will buzz the earth in 2029 and, depending on the trajectory, may be on course for a direct hit seven years later, when Ben is approaching my age. Not an extinction event, but a possibly catastrophic collision, nonetheless. Then there are the collisions nearer to home. On September 11, 2001, I held Ben, barely a year old, and watched Air Force One roar over our oak tree on its way to a military base in Omaha. Since then, Steph and I have been confronting a nation, a world, which often seems unfamiliar, full of unexpected disappointments and fears. I worry that what for us is new will be commonplace for our children. I worry that they will live out their adult lives afraid of the sky.

"Hey Dad, over here!"

I get up and walk over to where Ben has discovered a small plant with interesting, reddish "berries." He wants to eat one, but I decide it might be best to look the plant up in my guide. His mother once made the mistake of tasting the nauseating sap of Snow-on-the-Mountain, because of its evocative name and pretty white-fringed leaves. Ben's plant turns out to be native pasture rose; I tell him its berries or hips are rich in vitamin C, and were used by pioneers and tribal people for food and medicine. Ben decides against eating one—anything that good for you can't be tasty.

But there are other senses to indulge here. Spencer discovers a tall, lanky-leafed plant topped by tiny bouquets of white-lavender flowers. At first I think this may be oldfield balsam, also known as cudweed or rabbit tobacco, and I'm about to tell the boys how members of this species have been used to ward off everything from canker sores to diarrhea to ghosts. Then Spencer picks off a couple of leaves and we all smell the mint. Mountain mint, to be specific, though like "mountain" elk and grizzly bear it is a native prairie species. I read to them from the guide, revealing that the Potawatomi tribe, for whom our home county in western Iowa is named, considered mountain mint tea a good pick-me-up. Spencer tucks a handful of leaves in his pocket and, during the coming days, will show them to his mother, inviting her to "pick-up the mountains."

Ben inquires next about a long-stemmed plant, topped with spiky spheres that neither boy can resist touching. It resembles a medieval mace, which is probably why it attracted Ben in the first place. When I tell them the name—rattlesnake master— I'm hit with a barrage of questions:

"Does it bite?"

"Is it poisonous?"

"Does it turn into a rattlesnake when the moon is full?"

"Can you use it to hypnotize snakes and make them chase away girls?"

Actually, it was used to treat snakebites, I tell them, and I can see the disappointment in their eyes—more medicine. What I don't tell them is that rattlesnake master was also used to treat sexual exhaustion, a kind of Viagra of the prairie. Yet another fear to put off until the future.

"Isn't this bluestem?" Steph asks, pointing to a bunch of thigh-high grass. "Your favorite, right?"

She's right: It is bluestem and it is my favorite. It's also called turkey foot because of its three-toed cluster of flowers, but those won't develop until the late summer or fall, when the grass reaches six to nine feet. Its great height is one of the reasons I first admired it along country roads near Belle Plaine, and still do—some things haven't changed since my junior high days in Fort Dodge. The tall still rule. But in the years since Belle Plaine, I've come to admire bluestem for the other messages it drops at my feet. I reach down to dig my fingertips into the dense sod and touch a few of the plant's rhizomes and stolons, part of a massive web of interconnections that give this grass its paradoxical strength. Most of its living body is underground, intimately linked, impervious to and sustained by what might be considered merely destructive—fire, wind, ice, flood. During a drought, like now, it is never wasteful, saving every drop of water. At the same time, it does not hoard its treasure; it gives back to the soil, enriching and strengthening it, as well as the creatures who consume the grass itself. Bluestem provides protective shade for its offspring, which have learned to thrive in limited circumstances. Entwined with place, with its family and community, an individual plant may live half a century—longer than some trees, some people.

In contrast, there is Kentucky bluegrass, a large patch of which I spot nearby, its tall, droopy seed heads tossing in the breeze. It's an invasive, cool-season grass, which means it gets a jump start on most of the warm-season natives. When I get closer, I see that it is occupying the top of a Mima mound. There are over a hundred of these mysterious mounds at Kalsow, this one being around two feet high and twelve feet in diameter, though they can get larger. No one knows exactly how Mima mounds are formed, though it is likely by a combination of animal digging, frost heaves, and dust blown in from the surrounding fields, caught by the elevated earth. This process is not that different from the formation of the two-hundred-foot-high Loess Hills, where we live now, which were created by wind-blown, glacial silt—another collision, of sorts. But unlike those ancient formations, Mima mounds are collecting grounds for species not native to the area, such as Kentucky bluegrass. John Madson described Kalsow's Mima mounds as "a sort of Ellis Island of the prairie world," "intense isolated loci of disturbance," a "beachhead" for "foreign invaders." The risks for a small prairie like this are significant: Over time, bluegrass can push out most of the resident species. Once that happens, it may take over two hundred years to bring them back.

Beneath the surface, however, might be a different story. Mima mounds were once thought to be Indian burial grounds, but as Madson pointed out, excavations never uncovered bones or other signs of death. Only life. Toads, thousands of them, have been known to hibernate in the loose soil of these mounds. To them, it's no Ellis Island, no intense loci of disturbance. It's home.

Ben lets out another wail: "He hit me!" The king of the sky has struck again, this time with a stalk of rattlesnake master. Spencer has had a rough week. Last Wednesday, he was grounded, or "separated" as he calls it, for clawing one of neighbor Todd's four children. We have temporarily banned him from playing at their house, with its massive play set and (finally) terraced front yard, until he demonstrates he can act civilized. This latest incident has not helped his cause, and he knows it. He marches off defiantly into the deep grass and disappears. Seeking sanctuary in nature is nothing unusual for Spencer. Many times we've found him, completely naked, in the woods out back or in a tree or in the prairie garden out front. He's proven more willing than the rest of us to risk intimacy with the natural world, which sometimes leads to trouble: poison ivy, splinters, wasp stings, rocks dropped on toes. Other times, though, he has led us to amazing discoveries. Not just the usual earthworms and roly-poly colonies hidden beneath rocks, but also a woodchuck burrow, a newborn fawn, a hawk's nest, a log full of squirming red-bellied snakes. He has discovered injured birds and squirrels and butterflies, which we have done our best to nurse back to health or provide with a decent funeral. When we let him explore, naked or otherwise, chances are he will lead us to some new astonishment or responsibility we hadn't guessed was so close by.

It takes me a while to spot the crown of Spencer's blond head, nearly hidden in a thicket of sloughgrass. I'm unsure what, if anything, I can say about his behavior that will be helpful, so I talk about the grass instead. I congratulate him on choosing an amazing species to hide in, telling him that sloughgrass loves water more than any other prairie grass, and is the fastest-growing—sometimes reaching nine feet. To illustrate, I raise my hand as far as possible above my head. He turns to look, so I pull out all the stops, exclaiming how sloughgrass likes to hang out along the boggy potholes left over from when a glacier, a ginormous river of ice, way taller than our house, melted thousands of years ago. I tell him that this whole area was full of these potholes, inspiring one settler to name the nearby town of Moorland after the Scottish moors.

At this last detail he glazes over, but I continue, bravely: "Did you know, Spence, that the pioneers used to call this grass 'black-grass' because of its deep green color, and also because it marked wet places where their wagons might get stuck, the way our car did last spring in the mudhole at the end of the drive? Remember?"

"That's when you used the F word."

I ignore this and invite him to dig his hand into the sod at the base of the grass, denser even than the bluestem's, and to my surprise he does. I tell him that the pioneers thought it was the best thing for building sod houses and that many prairie Indians thought the leaves were the best thing for thatching the roofs on their lodges, to keep the rain and the snow from falling on their heads. I tell him that this place, where the glacier melted, where the sloughgrass grows, where his ancestors settled, where his father was raised, is the youngest of all the kinds of land in Iowa, just as he is the youngest in our family, and is the best place to grow things.

"The best place to grow up?" he asks.

I pause to consider the question.

"*Aaaieeeahh!*" Spencer charges out of the thicket, crying and holding his hand. "The grass cut me! The grass cut me and it's *bleeding!*"

Steph and Ben run over and we examine the wound, a fine cut at the base of the thumb. Nothing major, but a bleeder nonetheless.

"Don't touch it!" Spencer screams.

I tell Steph that I forgot to warn him about the serrated edges of sloughgrass, the reason farmers call it "ripgut."

"How could you forget that?" Ben chimes in, apparently forgetting the fresh welts on his back. "He's little and doesn't know any better."

"Yeah, I'm *little*," Spencer sobs, "and you should've *told* me! It's your fault and you need to get *separated*! *Aaaieeeahh . . .*"

"Now, now, Spence," I say, trying to redeem the situation. "Look at it this way: You've become blood brothers with the prairie."

"I don't *want* to be blood brothers with the prairie! I just want it to stop *hurting* and I want you to get *separated*!"

Steph gives me a sympathetic look that also suggests I should wander off for a moment, while she calms Spencer down.

So that's what I do. As I walk, I spot several familiar grasses and flowers from that first, flooded summer in Belle Plaine. I noticed many of them during the drive here as well, along the roadsides on the outskirts of Fort Dodge, which were lush and beautiful. Local citizens have been restoring those roadsides to native prairie, I hear, and I wonder how that effort has influenced a younger generation's relationship to home, if at all. Do they yearn as much as I did to leave, to experience more grandeur, more wildness? I feel it even now, on this prairie, which is nothing close to some of the others I've seen, with their thousands of acres of native grass teeming with wildlife. This place is so quiet, so small. Then again, why do I presume that a prairie, unlike a mountain, an ocean, or a human life, will roll out the entirety of its secrets for me, after neglecting it for a lifetime?

I walk farther, into deeper grass, and hear something: a soft, rhythmic clucking. Pheasants. *What is it with me and these birds?* I believe they may be following me, the way the crocodile followed Captain Hook, so I retreat to the top of a Mima mound. I try to spot them, but they remain hidden in the grass—they aren't going to give away any secrets either. I take the opportunity to look around, because whatever else might be said about Mima mounds, they offer perspective. The setting sun is getting ready to emerge from beneath the clouds. The storm I thought would chase us away has moved east over Fort Dodge, an indistinct darkness, until lightning illuminates the deep billows and folds of the clouds. Storm clouds here can reach forty thousand feet—powerful enough to tear jetliners apart, level entire towns, and also nourish this prairie, which will always welcome what the restless sky has to offer.

What did such a place hold inside my great-grandmother's gaze? Esther had no story to tell about that, but maybe I do. Both of us had come to the grasslands for the first time in our twenties, both from European landscapes—across the sea, and just down the road. We had both brought with us unrealistic expectations for this place and for ourselves, dreams and grievances that would perhaps never be satisfied. We had mourned lost family, and felt lost ourselves, foreign, small, in need of sanctuary. We had sought solace in nature, in the affection of friends and relatives, of a spouse, of God. And in language, where the personal story can sometimes be elevated by song. This is the home we had come to share, where the land still displays the contrary impulses of our nature—to fly, to settle—played out in harmony. I want to believe that, like me, she saw something to hope for in that.

When the sun finally emerges, the prairie erupts in bright colors, diverse textures, shadows, and depths. Steph and the boys have noticed it, too. Ben has his arm around Spencer's shoulder; they are looking out at a place transformed. What do they think of what has been given to them? Will they consider the conditions of their upbringing to be limited, as I once did? I hope that the stories of those who have come before, the stories of the land itself, will give them some courage, or at least make them feel less alone. I hope that, wherever they live, they will someday be able to sing with confidence the old psalm: *My boundaries enclose a pleasant land; indeed, I have a goodly heritage.*

Something explodes out of the grass, and I stumble back onto the ground. It's the pheasants, a half dozen of them, including a large, audaciously painted male. They fly over the heads of Stephanie and Ben, who point at them and shout; then they veer sharply, disappearing into the tall corn. There's a sudden rustling behind me. Spencer emerges from the grass, breathless from running.

"Did you see the pheasants, Daddy?" he asks. I nod and he plops down in my lap. He hands me a coneflower. "I'm sorry I yelled at you."

"That's all right," I tell him, kissing the top of his head. "I'm sorry I didn't warn you about the grass."

"That's all right," he says, and holds up his hand to remind me. The wound has stopped bleeding, but it is still bright red, to match the butterfly milkweed, the rose berries, the feathered mask of the pheasant, the horizon.

"Can I stop being separated now?" he asks.

"Done," I say. "And what about me? Can I stop being separated?"

He pauses to consider the question.

"OK," he sighs, reaching back to touch my face. "Why not?"

SELECTED BUR OAK BOOKS OF INTEREST

*The Ecology and Management of
Prairies in the Central United States*
Chris Helzer

Enchanted by Prairie
Bill Witt and
Osha Gray Davidson

*An Illustrated Guide to
Iowa Prairie Plants*
Paul Christiansen and
Mark Müller

Out Home
John Madson

*Restoring the Tallgrass Prairie:
An Illustrated Manual for Iowa
and the Upper Midwest*
Shirley Shirley

Stories from under the Sky
John Madson

*The Tallgrass Prairie Center Guide
to Prairie Restoration in the
Upper Midwest*
Daryl Smith, Dave Williams,
Greg Houseal, and
Kirk Henderson

*The Tallgrass Prairie Center Guide
to Seed and Seedling Identification
in the Upper Midwest*
Dave Williams

*Up on the River: People and Wildlife
of the Upper Mississippi*
John Madson

*Where the Sky Began:
Land of the Tallgrass Prairie*
John Madson

*Wildflowers and Other Plants
of Iowa Wetlands*
Sylvan T. Runkel and
Dean M. Roosa

Wildflowers of Iowa Woodlands
Sylvan T. Runkel and
Alvin F. Bull

*Wildflowers of the Tallgrass Prairie:
The Upper Midwest*
Sylvan T. Runkel and
Dean M. Roosa